GOD'S DESIGN® FOR THE PHYSICAL WORLD

INVENTIONS & TECHNOLOGY

D0814315

3RD EDITION | UPDATED, EXPANDED & FULL COLOR

ANSWERS IN GENESIS SCIENCE BY DEBBIE & RICHARD LAWRENCE

God's Design® for the Physical World is a complete physical science curriculum for grades 3–8. The books in this series are designed for use in the Christian school and homeschool, and provide easy-to-use lessons that will encourage children to see God's hand in everything around them.

Third edition
Third printing February 2012

ISBN: 1-60092-157-4

Cover design: Brandie Lucas
Layout: Diane King
Editors: Lori Jaworski, Gary Vaterlaus

Published by Answers in Genesis, 2800 Bullittsburg Church Rd., Petersburg KY 41080

Printed in China

www.answersingenesis.org • www.godsdesignscience.com

PHOTO CREDITS

TABLE OF CONTENTS

WELCOME TO
GOD'S DESIGN®
FOR THE PHYSICAL WORLD

You are about to start an exciting series of lessons on physical science. *God's Design® for the Physical World* consists of three books: *Heat and Energy*, *Machines and Motion*, and *Inventions and Technology*. Each of these books will give you insight into how God designed and created our world and the universe in which we live.

No matter what grade you are in, third through eighth grade, you can use this book.

3rd–5th grade

Read the lesson and then do the activity in the ⬤ box (the worksheets will be provided by your teacher). After you complete the activity, test your understanding by answering the questions in the ▬ box. Be sure to read the special features and do the final project.

6th–8th grade

Read the lesson and then do the activity in the ⬤ box. After you complete the activity, test your understanding by answering the questions in the ▬ box. Also do the "Challenge" section in the ⬤ box. This part of the lesson will challenge you to do more advanced activities and learn additional interesting information. Be sure to read the special features and do the final project.

There are also unit quizzes and a final test to take.

Throughout this book you will see special icons like the one to the right. These icons tell you how the information in the lessons fit into the Seven C's of History: Creation, Corruption, Catastrophe, Confusion, Christ, Cross, Consummation. Your teacher will explain these to you.

When you truly understand how God has designed everything in our universe to work together, then you will enjoy the world around you even more. So let's get started!

UNIT 1

COMMUNICATIONS

Enter

PRINTING PRESS

Communications breakthrough

Why is the printing press one of the most important inventions of all time?

Words to know:

proof

platen

Challenge words:

font

Communication is very important. From the very beginning of time, God communicated with man, and His words and actions were written down so that later generations would know God's thoughts. Communication has taken many forms in different societies. All societies have oral communication. Talking is a major way of conveying information. Complete histories have been passed on from one generation to another through oral stories.

However, talking is not the only form of communication. Some societies have used drums or smoke signals to pass on information, but written communication is the primary way of passing information on from one place to another, and from one generation to the next. Information has been recorded on clay tablets from before the time of Abraham. Other civilizations have used stone, animal skin scrolls (called parchment), and papyrus scrolls to record information. All of the books of the Bible were recorded and faithfully copied on parchment scrolls for hundreds of years. Written information is vitally important to the passing on of knowledge. This is why one invention is considered the most important invention of the modern world, and perhaps the most important invention of all time. That invention is

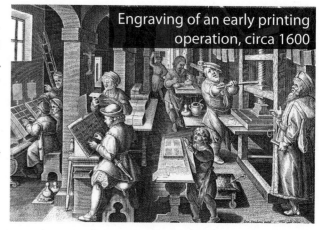

Engraving of an early printing operation, circa 1600

the printing press. The printing press allowed for the quick distribution of all kinds of information, and most importantly, the distribution of God's Word.

The invention of the printing press is credited to Johann Gutenberg who printed the first Bible on a letterpress from 1454–1457. Although block printing had existed in China for centuries, Gutenberg's press was the first to use metal moveable type.

A printing press involves three parts: the metal type, the ink, and the press. Perhaps the most difficult part of the invention was making the metal type. Each letter was made by first carving a mold, and then pouring molten metal into the mold. Gutenberg had worked as a metal punch maker earlier in his life, so he had the skills for designing and making the metal type needed for a printing press. Still, he worked for years to perfect the type-making process. Ink was already available, so once the type was perfected, the press had to be designed and built.

The process for printing a page was fairly long. First the letters for the words on one line were placed side by side on a composing stick. Next, the letters were transferred to a pan and held in place. When a whole page of words was ready, the letters were inked and a proof was made. A **proof** was a quick copy that was used to find any mistakes in the words. Once the letters were all placed correctly they were put into a frame and locked in place so they could not shift or fall out.

This frame was then placed in the press. The letters were inked using a leather ball that was filled with ink. Next, a piece of paper was placed over the inked letters. The **platen**, which was a thick piece of flat wood, was placed on top of the paper. The platen

MAKE YOUR OWN PRINTING PRESS

Purpose: To copy the process of the first printing press by using rubber stamps

Materials: rubber stamps, ink pad, paper, potato, knife, paint

Procedure:

1. Look at the bottom of the stamp. How does the word or picture appear? It looks backwards from what you expect. This is necessary in order to make the printed image correct.

2. Ink the stamp with an ink pad and press the stamp on a sheet of paper. You have just repeated the steps required for the printing press.

3. Use your stamps to make greeting cards to share with someone else.

Those students who are old enough to use a small knife can try making their own stamps. Stamps carved out of wood will last longer, but it is much harder and more time consuming to make them, so we will start by making stamps from pieces of a potato.

1. Decide what letter or design you wish to make.

2. Draw your design on a piece of paper and cut it out.

3. Place your design top side down on the potato.

4. Now, carefully carve away the potato from around your pattern, leaving the pattern sticking out.

5. Once you have your pattern, remove the paper, coat the stamp with tempera paint, and press it onto a piece of paper.

Conclusion: You have now made your first printing type. Making all the letters needed for a printing press was a long difficult process.

was then screwed down, pressing the paper tightly against the letters. The platen was then lifted and the paper removed and hung to dry. The letters were then re-inked and the process was repeated until the desired number of copies was made. When one page was completed, the letters were cleaned with an alkali solution and returned to the tray where they could be used in forming the next page.

Gutenberg's invention was so popular that it was quickly copied and improved upon. The invention of the printing press is largely responsible for the explosion of scientific discoveries, the Protestant Reformation, and the Renaissance, all of which occurred shortly after its invention.

Today, modern printing presses are wonders that can print thousands of pages in a very short period of time. Books, magazines, and newspapers are now abundant, and information is readily available in most parts of the world. The computer printer in your home or office is a direct descendant of Gutenberg's first printing press. ■

WHAT DID WE LEARN?

- What different forms of communication are commonly used?

- What was the very first human communication we know of?

- What are the three necessary parts of a printing press?

TAKING IT FURTHER

- Why is the printing press such an important invention?

- How are modern presses different from the original printing presses?

FONTS

As you know, all letters do not look alike. Not only does an "A" look different from an "E," but depending on the type of print you are using, an "A" can also look like **A**, A, **A** or *A*. Different styles of letters are called **fonts**. Some fonts are very plain and straight, while others are fancy and curly. Different fonts can give your writing a different look and feel. If you use a blocky font like this, **your writing will look very bold and straight**. If you want to have a more personal feeling to your writing, you might *use a font like this one.*

Research different fonts and make a poster showing what you have learned about the fonts that are commonly used in printing today. There are hundreds of different fonts, but most can be grouped into certain categories. Be sure to find out about serif, sans serif, calligraphy, and script categories of fonts.

JOHANN GUTENBERG

1394?–1468

For being one of the most important inventors of all time, we really know relatively little about Johann Gutenberg. We know that he was born sometime between 1394 and 1399, but his exact birth date is not known. He was born in Mainz in southwest Germany. Johann's parents were aristocrats (the noble ruling class), but their last name was Gensfleisch not Gutenberg. Gutenberg was the name of the house that they lived in and Johann was most likely called Johann von Gutenberg, meaning from Gutenberg, and the name stuck.

In 1428 there were riots against aristocrats in Mainz, so Johann and his parents fled to Strasbourg. There Johann worked making metal punches for gold working and polishing semiprecious stones. While doing this work, he had the idea of making letters that could be used in a press. He worked on molds that could be used to make lead letters. This was a painstaking process.

Eventually, Gutenberg set up his own shop with a couple of partners and began making mirrors and cheap jewelry. He used all of his extra earnings to finance his experiments with molds and metals. But by 1442, the business had dwindled and Johann was nearly bankrupt.

Gutenberg left Strasbourg and his whereabouts for the next four years are unknown. Then, in 1448, he returned to Mainz and set up a press on which he printed several copies of a grammar book called *Ars Grammatica*. This book was important to every scholar, but most people preferred the handwritten copies of the book. So Gutenberg continued working to perfect the printing process. Unfortunately, his expenses were greater than the profit he made on the few books that he printed, and he continued to have financial problems.

It seemed that his fortune was about to change in 1450, when a wealthy lawyer named Johann Fust decided to loan Gutenberg enough money to set up a real printing shop. To secure the loan, Gutenberg put all of his equipment up as collateral. Two years later the money had been used up and Gutenberg was still not making a profit, so he could not pay back the loan. Fust decided then to become a partner in Gutenberg's business. He contributed more money and encouraged Gutenberg to perfect the process so that they could begin making a profit.

By 1454 the process was good enough that Gutenberg set up 6 presses and began printing 200 copies of his now famous 42-line Bible. It took two years to complete and bind the first copy. During this time Fust decided to take Gutenberg to court and accused him of not paying back the original loan. The court sided with Fust and Johann lost all of his equipment and all of the copies of the Bible that were in progress. Fust and his son-in-law, who was also a partner in the business, made all of the profit from these first Bibles.

Gutenberg did not give up, however. He found a new partner, a wealthy man named Konrad Humery, who was willing to finance a new printing shop. It took three years for Gutenberg to build new molds, type, and presses. He then printed a new Bible in a different format from the earlier one. This new edition was very successful and allowed him to print many other works including a dictionary, an encyclopedia, and an astronomical calendar.

Gutenberg continued working on improving his presses and teaching apprentices until his death on February 3, 1468. Although we know little else about him, Gutenberg's contribution to the development of the movable type printing press changed the world.

This Gutenberg Bible is in the Thomas Jefferson Building at the Library of Congress. It is one of the finest copies still existing of the original 42-line Bibles. It is believed that between 180 and 200 of these Bibles were originally printed, and between 47 and 49 of them are still in existence today.

"It is a press, certainly, but a press from which shall flow in inexhaustible streams. . . . Through it, God will spread His Word. A spring of truth shall flow from it: like a new star it shall scatter the darkness of ignorance, and cause a light heretofore unknown to shine amongst men." – Johann Gutenberg

TELEGRAPH

Communication with wires

How can we communicate using wires?

Words to know:

telegraph key

telegraph receiver

Morse code

Although the invention of the printing press was extremely important for communications, it was not very efficient for getting a personal message from one place to another. Letters remained the major form of personal communication for hundreds of years after the printing press was invented. Shortly after electricity was first discovered, scientists began thinking of the many ways that electricity could be used to benefit mankind. However, it was a man with no scientific background who first developed a method for using electricity to send messages from one location to another.

Samuel F. B. Morse was an American painter with no training in science, but he was very interested in electricity. In 1832 Morse sketched out his first plan for an electromagnetic telegraph. He experimented with his ideas while working at New York University as an art teacher. On September 2, 1837, Morse conducted his first successful demonstration of the telegraph. He then decided to work with the lawmakers in Washington D.C. to build a full-fledged telegraph system, and in 1843 he convinced Congress to approve the first experimental transmission line. The wires were run from Baltimore, Maryland to Washington, D.C., along the tracks of the Baltimore and Ohio railroad.

The telegraph was first tested on May 1, 1844, even though the lines were not completely finished. Henry Clay had just received his party's nomination for president. This news was carried by a train from

> ## FUN FACT
>
> The Pony Express was the fastest way to get messages across the country until the invention of the telegraph. The telegraph ended the ride of the Pony Express.

Baltimore to where the telegraph line started. The message was then transmitted to Washington D.C. The train then continued on to Washington where the people on the train found that the message had arrived 1½ hours before the train did. The first official message was transmitted three weeks later from the Supreme Court chambers in Washington to Baltimore. The message that was sent was, "What hath God wrought!"

This successful transmission led to telegraph lines being installed across the country as well as along the bottom of the Atlantic Ocean to England. By 1866 over 100,000 miles (161,000 km) of telegraph wire had been installed. The major groups of people to first see the advantages of the telegraph were merchants, who could now send order and shipment information immediately, and journalists, who could now send news information anywhere in the country as soon as an important event took place.

The way that the telegraph works is quite interesting. First, a wire is stretched between two locations. At each location are a key and a telegraph receiver. The telegraph key is a metal switch like the one shown above, that can be pressed down against a wire to complete an electrical circuit. This causes current to flow through the wire. The telegraph receiver at the other location contains an electromagnet. As current flows through the wire, the receiver becomes magnetic and attracts a piece of metal to the magnet making an audible click. When the key is released, the current stops flowing and the receiver becomes nonmagnetic, releasing the piece of metal.

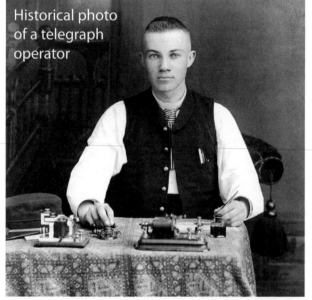

Historical photo of a telegraph operator

FUN FACT

Although the telegraph greatly improved the speed at which messages could travel across the country, there was still a limit to how fast a message could be sent. The best telegraph operators sent messages at only about 40 words per minute. In the next lesson we will learn about an invention that made communication even faster.

FUN FACT

Thomas Edison invented a way to send two telegraph messages at a time in each direction. This invention was called the duplex telegraph.

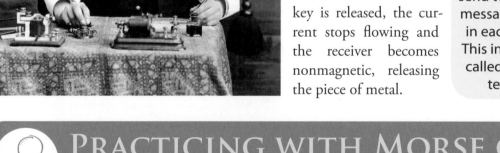

PRACTICING WITH MORSE CODE

Complete the puzzles on the "Morse Code Puzzles" worksheet by decoding each message.

The key can be pressed and released very quickly to send a series of electric pulses to the receiver. Morse developed a special code containing a series of short and long electrical signals that represented different letters or characters, called the Morse code. The short signals are referred to as dots and the long signals are called dashes. Each letter of the alphabet is represented by a different combination of dots and dashes, as shown below.

A •—	B —•••	C —•—•	D —••	E •	F ••—•
G ——•	H ••••	I ••	J •———	K —•—	L •—••
M ——	N —•	O ———	P •——•	Q ——•—	R •—•
S •••	T —	U ••—	V •••—	W •——	X —••—
Y —•——	Z ——••	0 —————	1 •————	2 ••———	3 •••——
4 ••••—	5 •••••	6 —••••	7 ——•••	8 ———••	9 ————•
Full stop (period) •—•—•—		Comma ——••——		Query (question mark) ••——••	

The telegraph operator at one location would use the key to send the signals to another location. At the other location, a second operator would listen to the series of clicks, decode the message, and deliver it to the appropriate person. ■

WHAT DID WE LEARN?

- What is the purpose of a telegraph system?
- What is the function of the telegraph key?
- What is the function of the receiver?
- What is Morse code?
- What is the difference between a dot and a dash in Morse code?
- Who is credited with inventing the telegraph?

TAKING IT FURTHER

- Why was the telegraph better than other methods of communication at that time?
- What changes do you think occurred in society because of the invention of the telegraph?

MORSE CODE

Practice tapping out long and short signals with your finger. Write your own message and tap it out on the table to a friend. Your friend should write down the dots and dashes and try to translate the message.

Special FEATURE

SAMUEL MORSE

1791–1872

An artist or an inventor—which was he? For most of his life, he and those who knew him would tell you that Samuel Morse was an artist. Born on April 27, 1791 in Charlestown, Massachusetts, he was one of eleven children, but only he and two younger brothers lived to adulthood. Jedidiah Morse, Samuel's father, was a minister and an author of the first American geography book. Jedidiah Morse's name was associated with geography the same way that his friend Noah Webster's name was associated with dictionaries. Also, Jedidiah was friends with George Washington.

When Samuel was 14 years old, he entered Yale College. He spent more time shooting and skating than studying. His father asked him to "use good sense," so because of his father's concern he settled down. Samuel enjoyed the lectures on electricity, but his real interest was drawing. Upon graduation, to please his parents, Samuel worked as a bookseller during the day, but he painted at night. His parents saw his talent and love for art, so with the help of some friends, they sent him off to London to study art. After four years, he returned to the United States and traveled around the country painting portraits. He made very little money at it; however, he did find a wife along the way. He married Lucretia Pickering in 1818, and together they had three children. She stayed with his parents while he traveled. Eventually, people recognized that Morse was one of America's finest

painters, and in 1819 he painted President Monroe's portrait and a painting of the House of Representatives.

In 1825 Lucretia died suddenly while he was away, but it was weeks before he found out. He was devastated. He returned to New York and bought a house, and he, along with a few other painters, started the National Academy of Design. He was still unable to make much money painting, so in 1829 he sold his house, left his children with family, and went to Italy to study. Three years later he returned. One evening, during dinner on the ship, the talk was about electromagnets and this gave Morse an idea. He spent the rest of the trip working on this new idea, and his work eventually produced the telegraph.

After returning to the U.S., Morse taught art at the University of New York for a time, but he eventually gave up art and concentrated on selling the telegraph. He met with many mishaps. At one of his demonstrations where he laid the line across the Hudson Bay, some fishermen pulled up his wire, and not knowing what it was, cut it in two and threw it back in the water. Finally, in 1843, Congress passed Morse's request to build his new invention. When he received the funds, he had two months to set up the lines between Baltimore and Washington D.C. He was successful and his days of living in poverty were over. Within 12 years, the telegraph was set up across the country and in Europe. He married again in 1848, and had three more children. Morse died in 1872.

TELEPHONE

Hello

LESSON

3

How does a telephone work?

Words to know:

telegram

microphone

Challenge words:

fiber optics

When was the last time you received a **telegram**? You have probably never received a telegraphed message. Although the telegraph was a revolutionary invention in 1844, experimentation with electricity and the movement of information did not stop there. The invention of the telephone has impacted lives even more than the invention of the telegraph, but the telegraph helped to spark the idea for the telephone.

Invention of the telephone

The invention of the telephone is credited to Alexander Graham Bell. Bell was born in Edinburgh, Scotland in 1847. Alexander's mother was mostly deaf, which inspired Alexander's great interest in the voice and how it is used for communication. He dedicated the greater part of his life to helping deaf people learn to communicate through speech.

Alexander was a natural inventor, and as a boy he designed a machine to help husk wheat. A few years later, he met a man who tried to make a machine to reproduce human speech. This intrigued Alexander, and he and his brother built a crude speaking machine. Alexander was also very interested in the telegraph and learned all he could about this interesting invention.

In 1870, after the deaths of both of his brothers to tuberculosis, Alexander's family decided to move to Canada. Alexander did not stay in Canada, but took a job in Boston where he worked with deaf students. Alexander's father had invented a system of symbols that represented all of the sounds of the spoken language, and Alexander used these to try to teach deaf children to speak.

As he studied more about the voice and the vibrations of the human throat, Bell began to think about ways to convert sound vibrations into electrical signals. Thus, the idea of the telephone was born. Alexander Graham Bell sent his first telephone message on March 10, 1876, when he used his invention to say, "Mr. Watson, come here, I want to see you." The early telephones could only be used in one direction. A message could be sent from one location and received in another, but not the other way around. Soon, however, the idea of two-way communication took hold, and transmitters and receivers were installed in both locations.

How telephones work

Although telephone technology has greatly improved, the ideas behind the telephone are still the same. Every telephone message begins with a microphone. The microphone translates the sound waves from your voice into electrical signals. Variations in your voice result in variations in the intensity and frequency of the electrical signal. The electrical signal travels through wires to another telephone where that phone's receiver converts the electrical signal back into sound waves in the speaker in the earpiece of the phone.

Getting a message from one location to another used to be a relatively simple process. One phone was directly wired to another. However, too many people wanted telephones for this to be a practical method, so switching mechanisms were invented to route and direct each phone message to the correct location. In

Historical photo of operators working a switchboard

> **FUN FACT**
>
> A man named Elisha Gray filed a claim for a patent for the invention of the telephone in 1876, just hours after Alexander Graham Bell filed for his patent, but Bell received the patent.

A SIMPLE TELEPHONE

Purpose: To make a simple telephone

Materials: two paper cups, string, paperclips

Procedure:

1. Using a pencil tip, punch a small hole in the bottom of a paper cup.

2. Thread a string through the hole and tie a paper clip to the end so the string does not pull back out.

3. Repeat this process with the other end of the string and a second cup.

4. Get a friend to take one end of the phone and you take the other.

5. Pull the string tight and take turns talking into the cup and listening to each other. You should be able to hear the person on the other end, even if they speak softly.

Questions: Explain how this homemade phone works. How is it similar to a real telephone?

the past, operators would switch the wires manually to connect callers (see photo on page 18). Today, your message may go through several calling exchanges electronically to reach its proper destination.

To connect with the person you wish to speak to, you first enter a number into your phone by pressing numbers on the keypad. This sends routing information ahead of your voice, so that the route is found. That route may be directly along telephone lines, or may include sending the information to a satellite, which then beams the message back to another location. Long distance calls and cellular phones often use satellites to direct their messages to the correct phone.

Mobile phones

You or your parents may have a mobile, or cell phone. These are handy portable phones that can be used almost anywhere. A cell phone is really a radio. It uses radio waves to transmit signals. Whereas a typical radio or walkie-talkie allows for one-way transmission of signals, cell phones operate on a duplex system, which uses two frequencies at the same time—one for talking and one for receiving. You will learn more about radios in the next lesson.

Cellular systems are made up of a series of geographical areas, called cells (thus the name of the phone). Within these cells are many assigned channels. These cells are connected by towers that send and receive signals. As you travel, the system automatically transfers your call from one cell to another, so that you're always in range of a tower. However, there are a few areas where there's too much distance between towers, usually in remote areas. When you get caught in one of those areas, the signal from your phone can't find a tower to receive it, and your call will drop.

The first cell phone technology was analog. However, this technology is limited due to the way that the signal is carried. The newest cell phones are digital. Digital phones use binary code (0s and 1s) and compress the data to fit more calls into a given frequency. There can be between three and ten calls per frequency, whereas analog phones only allowed one.

What is in the future for telephones? We can't be sure. But if the recent past is any indication, companies will continue to come up with new ways for us to communicate, and phones will have more and more features. ■

WHAT DID WE LEARN?

- What are the major functions of a telephone?
- What is the function of the keypad on a telephone?
- Who is credited with inventing the telephone?
- What is a cell phone?

TAKING IT FURTHER

- How did Alexander Graham Bell's work with deaf children influence his invention of the telephone?
- How does a cellular phone operate differently from a regular telephone?

FIBER OPTICS

For many years, all telephone signals traveled from one place to another on metal wires, but today, many phone systems use fiber optic cables instead. With a fiber optics system there is no difference in your home—the sound is still translated into electrical signals by your telephone. But once the electrical signal leaves your home, it may be converted into pulses of light that travel along tiny glass fibers. Fiber optic signals travel more quickly than electrical signals and are more accurate.

A **fiber optic** cable consists of hundreds of very thin clear glass fibers. Each fiber consists of a glass core that is coated with a reflective surface. This allows light to be reflected along the inside of the cable without interfering with neighboring cables. Messages are sent as pulses of light that are generated by a laser. Each fiber can carry thousands of calls at one time.

Fiber optics is a major advancement in communication technology.

Purpose: To simulate fiber optics by building your own "optical cable"

Materials: cardboard box, black paint, flexible plastic tubing, modeling clay, plastic wrap, tape, flashlight

Procedure:

1. Paint the inside of a box black.

2. Cut a small hole near the bottom of one side of the box. The hole must be just big enough for a piece of flexible tubing to slide through it.

3. Cut a piece of plastic tubing 8 to 12 inches long.

4. Tape plastic wrap over one end and fill the tube with water.

5. Push the covered end of the tube inside the box.

6. Press modeling clay around the tube on both the inside and outside of the box to form a light-tight seal.

7. Arrange the tube inside the box so that the covered end is pointing up.

8. Darken the room and shine a flashlight into the open end of the tube. If you cannot darken the room, cover your head and the box so that no outside light gets in.

Conclusion: You should be able to observe the light from the flashlight shine out of the covered end of the tube. The light travels through the water in the tube just as it does down a fiber optic cable.

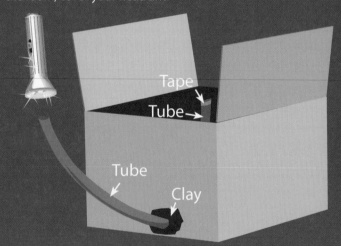

RADIO

No wires

LESSON

4

How does a radio work without wires?

Words to know:

modulation

amplitude modulated

frequency modulated

amplifier

tuner

analog

digital

Challenge words:

resonance

The telegraph made it so that people could send messages across the country in a very short period of time. The telephone enabled people to talk to each other from different locations. But both the telephone and telegraph required that electrical wire be run from one location to the other. Several scientists did research trying to find a way to send information without the use of wires. The result was radio.

Heinrich Hertz was the first scientist to discover radio waves. He made this discovery in 1888. Only six years later, another scientist, Oliver Lodge, sent the first radio message between two buildings. His message was sent in Morse code. However, the major work on radio transmission is credited to an Italian scientist named Guglielmo Marconi. Marconi began transmitting radio waves in 1896. He experimented with ways to transmit the waves over greater and greater distances. By early 1901, he was able to transmit radio waves over 200 miles. But Marconi's goal was to transmit across the ocean. Many people said this was impossible because of the curvature of the earth. However, Marconi was convinced that if he found the right locations he could transmit between North America and England. In December of 1901, Marconi, with the help of many others, set up two radio stations. The transmitter was set up in Poldhu, England. The receiver was set up in Newfoundland, Canada. The station in England continuously transmitted short bursts representing the letter "S" in Morse code. Due to severe weather in Newfoundland, it took a couple of days to get the receiving equipment to work, but Marconi and his helpers were able to detect the distinct tap-tap-tap of the code sent from England.

In 1906 a Canadian scientist named Reginald Fessenden developed a process called modulation, which allows the desired message to be added to a carrier radio signal. This allows for multiple radio signals to be broadcast at the same time, while a receiver can tune in only the desired signal.

Just like in a telephone, a radio message begins with a microphone that is used to translate sounds into electrical signals. For stereo sound, two separate microphones are used to make two slightly different copies of the sound. The radio transmitter then converts the electrical signal into a radio wave. This radio wave is combined with a high-speed carrier wave and sent out in all directions. AM radio signals are ones that are amplitude modulated. This means that the frequency of the carrier wave remains the same while the amplitude, or height, of the signal varies with the frequency and volume of the sound signal. FM radio signals are frequency modulated. This means that the amplitude of the signal remains the same, while the frequency of the carrier signal changes with the frequency and volume of the sound. Each radio station has an assigned carrier frequency at which it can transmit.

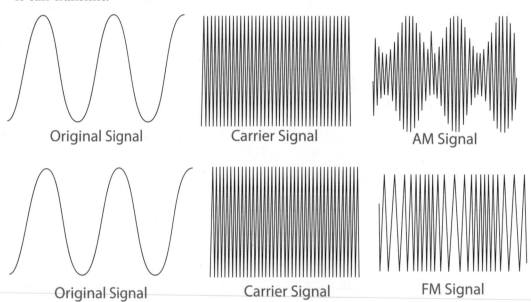

Original Signal   Carrier Signal   AM Signal

Original Signal   Carrier Signal   FM Signal

Radio signals can travel for hundreds or even thousands of miles if conditions are right. The distance that the signal travels depends in large part on the strength of the transmitted signal. The strength of a signal sent from a radio station is often limited so that its signal does not interfere with the signal from another radio station many miles away.

Your radio is designed to be a receiver. It receives the radio signal, removes the carrier signal, and then converts the remaining signal into an electrical signal. This signal is often weak, so an amplifier is used to boost the strength of the electrical signal, which in turn is converted by a speaker back into sound. Because there are many radio signals being transmitted at the same time, your radio must have a tuner that allows you to select the desired signal. Your radio has an antenna that vibrates as many radio signals hit it. Your tuner filters out all of the signals except the one you are interested in.

TRANSMITTING RADIO SIGNALS

Purpose: To transmit your own radio signals and detect them using a portable radio

Materials: electrical wire, tape, 6-volt battery, metal file, portable radio

Procedure:

1. To build your transmitter, first cut two pieces of electrical wire, each about 12 inches long and strip off about 1 inch of plastic from each end of each wire.

2. Tape the end of one wire to the negative terminal of a 6-volt battery and the end of the second wire to the positive terminal of the battery.

3. Tape the free end of the first wire to the end of a metal file. Now you can rub the free end of the second wire across the file to complete the circuit and cause electrons to flow. This is your transmitter.

4. Set a portable radio near the file, turn it on and tune it to an AM radio station.

5. Now brush your wire across the file. This creates little crackles of sound that are picked up by the radio.

You are transmitting a signal to the radio. It is not a very pretty sound, but it demonstrates how the radio transmitter works. Just be glad that real transmitters send out more than crackles.

Many sound signals are transmitted as analog signals. Analog signals are continuous. But more recently, many signals are being sent as digital signals. Digital signals convert the information into a series of pulses. Digital information is more accurate because it is either on or off and cannot be distorted by background noise. Today, both digital and analog radio continue to play a large role in the distribution of information and entertainment. ■

WHAT DID WE LEARN?

- Who is the person most responsible for developing radio?
- What are the main parts of a radio system?
- What is the function of each of these parts?

TAKING IT FURTHER

- Why does a digital signal give you a better sound than an analog signal?
- What is an advantage of using a radio to send a message over using a traditional telephone?
- Under what conditions might you choose to use a radio to contact someone?
- What is the main thing radio is used for today?

TUNER MODEL

Being able to filter out unwanted radio signals is very important to receiving a good sound on your radio. The tuner allows you to do this. Inside the tuner are various electrical circuits that vibrate at given frequencies. When the antenna vibrates at the same frequency that a particular circuit naturally vibrates at, that circuit begins to vibrate and produce sound. To better visualize how this works you can build a tuner model.

Purpose: To build a model of a tuner

Materials: string, modeling clay, table, "Radio Tuner" worksheet

Procedure:

1. Tie a piece of string tightly between two table legs.

2. Cut five pieces of string in the following lengths: 5 inches, 10 inches, 15 inches, 15 inches, and 20 inches.

3. Tie each of the strings to the string you placed between the table legs at 2-inch intervals.

4. Attach a 1-inch diameter ball of clay to the end of one of the 15-inch strings.

5. Attach a different color ball of clay to the end of each of the other four strings. The first 15-inch string represents your tuner. The strings with the second color of clay represent different radio signals.

6. Now, use each string as a pendulum. Pull the 5-inch string out a short distance and let it swing back and forth. Watch the tuner string for any vibrations. Write your observations on a copy of the "Radio Tuner" worksheet.

7. Stop the first string and set the 10-inch string in motion. Again, watch the tuner for movements and record your observations on your worksheet.

8. Repeat with each of the other strings.

Conclusion:

What did you find? Only the 15-inch string should cause the tuner string to begin swinging. Each string has a natural frequency at which it vibrates. The tuner will begin to vibrate when it is close to something that is vibrating at its natural frequency. This is called **resonance** and is how the tuner works in your radio.

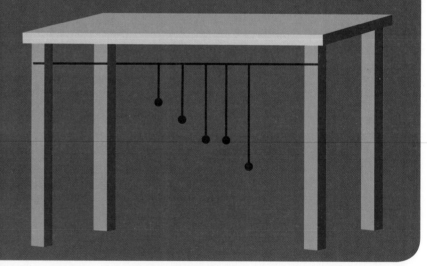

TELEVISION

Pictures in your home

How can pictures be transmitted through air?

Words to know:

CRT/cathode ray tube

pixel/picture element

liquid crystal display/ LCD

plasma display

Shortly after the invention of radio, many scientists quickly turned their attention to developing a system that would send not only sound, but also pictures over radio waves. This system was later to be called television. The first scientist to send both sound and pictures using radio waves was John Baird in 1924. However, his system was mechanical rather than electrical and had very poor quality. Scientists from AT&T sent the first electronically-generated television signal from New York to Washington D.C. in 1927. The first regularly-scheduled television programming began in 1928, and the first broadcast of color television was in 1941. Since that time, television has grown into one of the primary sources of information and entertainment in the world. Television has had a profound impact on nearly every society.

The television signal

Receiving a television signal at your house is a somewhat more complicated process than the process needed for sending and receiving radio signals because of the complexity of sending and receiving visual images. First, in addition to a microphone to pick up sound, a television camera is needed to record the images that are to be sent. A television camera uses a lens to focus the image onto a series of electrical devices that are sensitive to light. Three sets of devices are used. One set is sensitive to red light, another is sensitive to green light, and the third is sensitive to blue light. These devices change the image into an electrical signal containing red, green, and blue information. A microphone is used to change the sound into an electrical signal at the same time. All of these signals are combined together with a carrier signal just like radio signals and are then transmitted through the air. Local TV signals, such as a local news show, are transmitted directly to your home. Other signals, such as a presidential speech, may be transmitted to satellites that are orbiting the earth. These satellites then retransmit the signal to satellite dishes at your local station, and then are transmitted to your home. Other TV signals are transmitted over television cables instead of on radio waves. Television cables may be metal or fiber optic.

Forming the picture

Regardless of how the signal gets to your TV, your TV set must then change the radio signal or electrical signal back into picture and sound. Inside a traditional TV is a large tube called the picture tube. The more scientific name for this tube is a CRT, or cathode ray tube. The front surface of the CRT is the screen that you watch. The inside of the screen is coated with thousands of tiny dots of chemicals called phosphors, which glow when hit by electrons. Some phosphors glow red, some glow green, and others

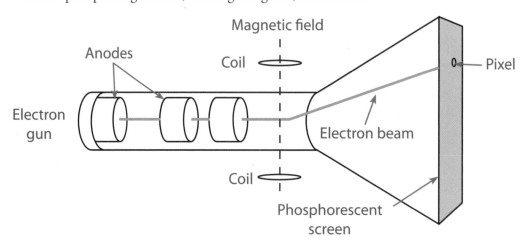

glow blue. Each dot is referred to as a pixel, which is short for picture element.

Recall that the signal that is sent has information about how much red, green, and blue is in the image at each instant. This information is used to fire beams of electrons at the different dots on the screen to turn them on. The guns that fire the electrons sweep across the screen from top to bottom about 30 times per second,

COMBINING LIGHT

Colored television images are composed of just three colors: red, green, and blue. These three colors of light can be combined in different combinations and different intensities to produce all of the colors you see on your TV screen. Hold pieces of red, green, and blue cellophane or plastic wrap in front of a flashlight. Point the light at a white wall. See how many different colors of light you can produce using the different colors of cellophane.

changing the pixels that are lit up with each sweep. The picture on the screen is not really a single image, but actually a series of dots that change so quickly that your eyes and brain merge them into a single, smoothly moving image. You can see these dots if you look at your TV screen with a magnifying glass.

The signal that is received by your TV also contains sound information. This signal is sent to your TV's speaker where it is changed back into sound so you hear the sound at the same time that you see the image.

Some of the newer televisions have thin flat-panel screens. These TVs do not have a picture tube as described above. Instead, they have a liquid crystal display (LCD) or a plasma display. These types of screens are made with special materials that react to electrical current in predictable ways. Thus, they can use the information in the TV signal to recreate the picture, but they are much flatter than the traditional television set.

HDTV

The information that is transmitted from a TV station used to be transmitted as an analog signal, similar to the way radio signals have been transmitted. However, the U.S. government mandated that in 2009 all television stations were to begin transmitting TV signals in a digital format. This new format is called HDTV, which stands for High Definition Television.

HDTV has many advantages over traditional analog TV signals. First, it is a clear signal; it does not pick up interference like an analog signal can. Second, the HDTV format gives you a much more detailed picture. A standard TV has 480 lines from top to bottom, but an HDTV has either 720 or 1080 lines from top to bottom. There are approximately twice as many lines in the vertical direction as well, giving the viewer of a 1080 signal about four times as many dots on the screen, which makes the picture much clearer and sharper than an analog picture.

The HDTV format also has a different shape from the standard TV. The standard TV format has four dots across for every three dots down. The HDTV format has 16 dots across for every 9 dots down. Thus the new HDTV is wider than the traditional TV screen. This is similar to the shape of the screen at a movie theater.

The sound signal that is transmitted with the new HDTV signal is also better than the traditional sound signals. The new digital

TVs have changed a lot over the years.

sound signals have information that is compatible with Dolby digital surround sound. HDTV will greatly improve both the picture and the sound quality for televisions.

Most newer televisions, those sold after March 2007, are required to have a digital TV tuner that can receive the HDTV signals or to alert the customer that the TV will not be HDTV compatible. However, people with older, analog TVs need to purchase a digital-to-analog converter to connect to their TV if they wish to receive TV signals. ∎

WHAT DID WE LEARN?

- How is a television different from a radio?

- What is the picture tube in a traditional TV properly called?

- What kind of information is transmitted by TV stations?

- How does your TV produce a visual image on the screen?

TAKING IT FURTHER

- How do you think your TV changes stations?

- Why do you see a complete image when there are really just thousands of little red, green, and blue dots on the screen?

- What are some advantages that HDTV has over traditional TV?

REMOTE CONTROL

Most television sets produced today have more circuitry than just that required for receiving and producing the sounds and images you want to see. Most TVs also come with a remote control device.

A remote control is used to tell the TV what you want it to do. Each button on the remote closes an electrical circuit inside the device causing it to emit a particular radio signal. A receiver inside the television receives and interprets the signal and sends electrical commands to the TV's circuitry causing it to respond in a programmed way.

For example, if you push the power button, a signal is sent to the TV and its receiver sends a signal to the power switch causing it to change to the opposite position, either turning the TV on or off. Other signals cause the TV to change to a different channel or adjust the volume of the sound.

If you have access to a TV remote control, test it to find where the signal is transmitted from. Also, try to find where the TV receives the signal. Generally, the remote needs to be pointed at the TV for it to work well because the signals produced are relatively weak and sent in only one direction, so you don't accidentally control your neighbor's TV set.

Try pointing the remote away from the TV. Try bouncing the signal off of a wall or window. Also, try covering up the receiver on the TV to see if it makes any difference in how well the remote works. You may want to try to determine what each button does on your remote.

Some remote control devices are very simple and others are very complex.

FAX MACHINE

Sending a copy

LESSON 6

What is a fax machine?

Words to know:

fax/facsimile

resolution

Most inventions in communication owe their beginnings to the telegraph, and the fax machine is no exception. The word **fax** is short for **facsimile**, which means an exact copy. And shortly after Morse successfully demonstrated his electronic telegraph, a Scottish mechanic named Alexander Bain began working on a way to electronically send copies of the written word. Bain received a patent for his invention, which was described as an electric printing and signal telegraph, in 1843. This device used a series of pendulums to simulate the movements of a pen for writing and changed the movement of a pen into electrical signals. This is very different from the fax machines of today, but it began the research and development necessary to lead to what we have today.

In 1902 Arthur Korn of Germany developed a photoelectric system that used light-sensitive materials to change a photograph into electrical signals that could be transmitted over telegraph wires. Korn conducted the first intracity transmission of a photograph in 1907, when he sent a photo from Munich to Berlin. Then, in 1925, a French inventor named Edouard Belin invented a machine that functions very similarly to today's fax machines. This machine used a cylinder to move the image. A powerful light scanned the image and a photoelectric

SENDING A FAX

A fax machine reproduces an image in a similar way to how a television reproduces an image. It scans the page line by line and breaks the image up into tiny squares, similar to the dots on a TV screen.

Purpose: To visualize how a fax machine works

Materials: "Fax Machine Template," black pen or pencil

Procedure:

1. Make two copies of the "Fax Machine Template."

2. On one copy, draw a simple letter, number, or other picture that is large enough to mostly fill the "screen" of the fax machine.

3. Color the figure black.

4. Have one person send this message to the other by doing the following:

   A. The receiver should have a blank copy of the "Fax Machine Template."

   B. The sender should look at each square of the image being sent and starting with A1, examine the box. If the box is more than 50% filled in tell the receiver that it is black. If it less than 50% filled in tell the receiver that the box is white. Next move on to location A2 and tell the receiver if the box is black or white. Repeat for each square on the fax machine.

   C. The receiver should color each box black if the sender says it is black and leave it white if it is white.

   D. After you have "scanned" the entire screen, compare the image that was sent to the image that was received.

The received image will not be an exact copy because the size of the squares is very large compared to the size of the image. This means that your fax machine has very low resolution. **Resolution** is the number of pixels or pieces of information that an image is broken into. You only broke the image up into 64 squares. A good fax machine breaks the image up into more than 2 million squares. The smaller the squares, the better the received image will look.

circuit converted the light or absence of light into electrical signals that could be transmitted.

In 1934 the Associated Press began using this technology to send news photos across the country. By the 1960s, fax machines were becoming somewhat common in many offices, but they were bulky and expensive. As technology developed, the machines became much smaller and much faster. In 1973 there were approximately 30,000 fax machines in use. By 1983 there were nearly 300,000 machines in use, and in 1989 that number had grown to over a million. Today, most businesses and many homes have fax machines to enable them to send copies of papers and pictures to anyone who has a phone line and another fax machine.

Similar to the telegraph, telephone, and radio, the fax

FUN FACT

The patent for the fax machine was granted 33 years before a patent was granted for the telephone. Remember, the first fax machine used telegraph wires, not phone lines.

machine consists of transmission circuitry and receiving circuitry. The transmission part of the fax machine basically scans the images on a sheet of paper using a laser beam. This light is reflected to photoelectric circuitry that detects light and dark areas, converting this information into electrical signals that can be transmitted on the telephone wires. At the other end of the telephone line, a second fax machine receives the electrical signals. The receiver converts the electrical signal into a picture causing the image to be reproduced on a piece of paper.

Fax machines are used for many purposes including sending legal documents instantly. ■

WHAT DID WE LEARN?

- What does fax mean?
- What is the purpose of a fax machine?
- How does a fax machine send a copy of an image?

TAKING IT FURTHER

- Why might a business use a fax machine?
- How is a fax machine similar to a telephone?
- How is a fax machine different from a telephone?
- What technology is replacing some of the job of a fax machine?

INCREASING RESOLUTION

If you are sending an image that has nice straight edges, you may get a pretty good copy even if your resolution is pretty low. However, sending a circle becomes more difficult. If you want your copy to look like a circle, you must make your resolution much higher—that means your squares have to be much smaller.

Experiment with different sized squares for your simulated fax machine. Begin by dividing each square into four squares. This will give you 256 squares. If you are still not satisfied with the results, try dividing each of those squares into four squares. How small do you need to make your squares in order for the copy to look like a circle?

Use a magnifying glass to examine a copy of an image that was received by a fax machine. If you do not have access to a faxed image, look at a newspaper. Examine the letters and images with straight lines to see how straight they look when enlarged by the magnifying glass. Also, look at the round letters and images to see how smooth the edges appear. The magnifying glass should show you that the image is not completely smooth.

COMPUTER

The ultimate in communications?

LESSON 7

How did we ever get along without computers?

Words to know:

abacus

CPU/central processing unit

RAM

hard drive

hardware

software

Today it is hard to imagine having to wait weeks to hear from a loved one in another state, or never owning a book because it was too expensive. We live in what is often called the information age. Information is readily available to nearly everyone. From local libraries to the Internet, people can communicate with each other instantly and can find out about nearly any topic at the press of a button or by checking out a book. All of this is due to the development of the computer.

When you think of a computer what do you think of? You probably think of a machine that allows you to type up a school report, look up information on the Internet, or email a friend. You might even think of video games. But the computer was invented to do mathematical calculations very quickly. All of the other uses for a computer grew out of its ability to do math.

Someone did not just decide one day to build a new invention and call it a computer. The computer was the result of a long line of inventions before it. The discovery of electricity was the real catalyst for many of the inventions of the 19th and 20th centuries. Without electricity, we would not have telephones, televisions, or computers. However, there were many mechanical devices that did calculations before the invention of what we think of as a computer today.

Going back to ancient times, people used the **abacus**, a simple mechanism with beads like the one shown here

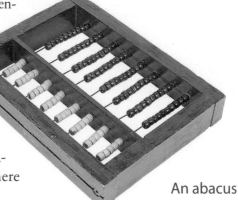

An abacus

that aided in doing mathematical calculations. The first working mechanical calculator was created by Charles Babbage in 1832. It used a series of over 2,000 gears. The first electronic programmable calculator was created by a German scientist named Konrad Zuse in 1941. Then, in 1947, Bell Labs invented the transistor, which revolutionized the electronics industry and made computers practical.

The first all electronic computer was huge! Built in 1946, the Electronic Numerical Integrator and Computer, ENIAC for short, weighed nearly 30 tons, measured 8.5 feet (2.6 m) by 3 feet (0.9 m) by 80 feet (26 m), and had miles of wiring. As amazing as this computer was, it can't compare to today's desktop computers. The ENIAC could only store 200 digits. Today's computers can store more than16 million digits. In addition, many of today's computers are 60,000 times faster than ENIAC was. Even some calculators that would fit in your pocket are more powerful than the gigantic ENIAC.

The final invention that really made computers available to the everyday person was the invention of the integrated circuit by both Texas Instruments and Fairchild Semiconductor in 1959. Since that time, computers have become smaller, more powerful, and less expensive each year, until today nearly every household in the United States owns a computer.

There are many parts of a computer system and we could spend many lessons learning about them all, but in this lesson we will look at the basics of what is inside the box we call a personal computer. The most important part of your computer is

Replica of a portion of Babbage's machine

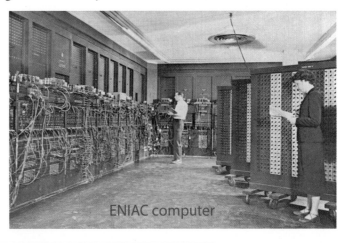

ENIAC computer

FUN FACT

IBM's supercomputer, Blue Gene/L, which operates at Lawrence Livermore National Laboratory in California, is the world's fastest computer, able to make 280.6 trillion calculations per second.

There is an even better computer, but it's not made by man. It's sitting right on top of your shoulders! The human brain is an amazing computing device created by our powerful Creator. Your brain is made up of about one trillion cells with 100 trillion connections between those cells. The human brain is capable of handling at least 100 trillion calculations per second, and all within a package just 56 cubic inches (918 cubic centimeters) in volume that weighs 3.3 pounds (1.5 kg). Blue Gene/L takes up 320 square feet (30 square meters) of floor space and weighs more than 1,000 pounds (450 kg)! We are truly an amazing creation of God.

COMPUTERS IN ACTION

Think about all the ways computers affect your life. Remember that computers are not only used in homes, but are used in nearly every area of life. Make a list of some of the ways that computers affect you. List how computers are used in your home, how they are used in places that you visit, and how they are used by people who do things for you. Your list could be very long if you tried to list everything, but try to list at least 10–15 ways that computers are used around you.

your **CPU**—**central processing unit**. The CPU is the brain of the computer. It is the part of the computer that does most of the calculations and tells the other parts of the computer what to do.

Your computer also has memory inside. **RAM**, or random access memory, is for storing short-term information. RAM holds commands and data that will be used soon or have been used recently by the CPU. The **hard drive** in your computer, on the other hand, is much larger and is used to store information indefinitely. This is where applications and documents are stored. A hard drive stores information in the form of tiny magnetic fields that can be detected by an electromagnet. Other types of storage include CDs, DVDs, and jump drives, but all of these can be moved from one computer to another, so they are not really part of your computer.

Your computer also contains circuitry to move information from the memory to the CPU and from all the devices that are connected to your computer including your monitor, printer, keyboard, and mouse. Depending on your computer, it may have circuitry that performs many other functions as well, including a graphics card that performs all of the calculations necessary to move images on the screen, a math

processing unit to more quickly perform mathematical calculations, and a sound card to change electrical signals into sound waves.

All of the information inside the computer is stored as a series of 1s and 0s. A 1 represents a pulse of electricity and a 0 represents no electricity. These pulses of electricity are like little keys that open and close gates inside your CPU to make things happen. You can think of a computer program a little bit like a very complex Morse code message. In Morse code, the dots and dashes represent letters, and in a computer, the 1s and 0s represent letters, symbols, and commands for the computer to perform.

Computer **hardware** refers to objects that you can actually touch, like disks, disk drives, display screens, keyboards, printers, boards, and memory chips. **Software**, on the other hand, exists as electronic information but it has no substance. A book provides a good analogy. The pages and the ink of the book are the hardware, while the words, sentences, paragraphs, and the overall meaning are the software. A computer without software is like a book full of blank pages—you need software to make the computer useful just as you need words to make a book meaningful.

Computers are undoubtedly one of the most important inventions ever. After the printing press, the computer has had more influence on our culture than any other communication device ever made. Of course, without the knowledge gained from inventing the telegraph, telephone, radio, and television, the computer would never have become the significant tool that it is today. ■

WHAT DID WE LEARN?

- What is the "brain" of a computer?
- What is RAM?
- What is RAM used for?
- What were computers designed for initially?
- What are some other functions of computers today?

TAKING IT FURTHER

- How are binary codes, 1s and 0s, similar to Morse code?
- What new application can you think of for a computer?
- What would you use a computer for if you could?

INPUT AND OUTPUT

The CPU inside your computer is pretty useless if you cannot communicate with it. So engineers have designed many ways to allow you to communicate with your CPU. You must be able to send information and commands to the CPU, and you must be able to get information back out. Information going into the CPU is called input, and information coming out is called output. Think about how you "talk" to a computer, and then complete the "Computer Architecture" worksheet.

The Internet

If you own a computer, you probably have the ability to use the Internet. The Internet is an amazing connection of computers around the world. With a connection to the Internet you have access to information about nearly anything. You can do a research paper, find a phone number, look up the local movie listings, chat with a friend anywhere in the world, shop, and many other things that we don't have room to mention.

The Internet was not invented by a single person, but has been developed as a joint effort, as well as competing efforts, by many people over the past 40 to 50 years. The first person recorded as having a vision for connecting computers together to share information was a researcher at the Massachusetts Institute of Technology (MIT) named J. C. R. Licklider who wrote a paper in 1962 suggesting the idea. After that time, scientists at MIT and the University of California at Los Angeles (UCLA) led the research on developing a way to connect computers in different locations together and providing a way for them to share information.

In 1965 a computer in Massachusetts was connected to a computer in California via telephone lines and the first "Internet" message was sent. This connection showed that telephone switching technology was not sufficient to handle the information transfers, so new technology had to be developed.

The first host computer that was designed to transfer information between other computers was set up at UCLA in 1969, and Charley Kline of Stanford University was the first to use this new network. The first email was sent in 1972 by Ray Tomlinson who worked for the research company Bolt Beranek and Newman (BBN).

Originally the Internet was established as a way for researchers and engineers to access and share data. The library systems were involved in storing data and making it available. The military became involved in using the Internet in 1980, and the government became more financially involved when the National Science Foundation funded the first backbone network of computers beginning in 1986.

The Internet was strictly for research and was not available to the public for many years. But as web browsers (software used to look up information) became more user-friendly, companies began to see the commercial possibilities of an Internet that was available to everyone.

Around 1992 companies began working on ways to make the Internet accessible to the public. The first graphical, easy-to-use interface was Mosaic, developed in 1993. Marc Andreessen, the developer of Mosaic, went on to develop Netscape, which was released to the public in 1994 and the Internet as we know it today was born.

Today, over 1 billion people have access to the Internet on a regular basis. People access the Internet at work and at home. But many other places are making the Internet available as well. You can access the Internet at many hotels and restaurants. You can even access the Internet at some rest stops. With so much information available, companies are designing new ways to access the Internet as well. You don't even need a computer. You might be able to use your PDA, cell phone, or GPS system to access the Internet. Or maybe you can even use your refrigerator!

The commercial Internet is only a little more than a decade old. It still has huge potential to change and grow. In the coming years we will see many new ways to exchange information and connect with people around the world.

UNIT 2

TRANSPORTATION

STEAM ENGINE

A new age of power

LESSON

8

How does a steam engine work?

The invention of the steam engine is credited with starting the Industrial Revolution. Prior to its invention, machines were powered by animals or by water wheels, but the steam engine paved the way for the use of machines in nearly every application imaginable. The Greeks used steam to power spinning balls and other toys, but did not harness the great power of steam.

The first practical use of steam was a steam-driven pump designed by Thomas Newcomen in 1712. Coal was used to heat water until it turned to steam. Water expands as it turns to steam and thus creates pressure inside the water tank. This pressure was released into a cylinder with a piston, thus pushing the piston up. Then the outside of the cylinder was cooled, cooling the steam and turning it back into water, which takes up less room than the steam. This created a vacuum inside the cylinder, pulling the piston back down. The up and down movement of the piston was used to move a rocker arm up and down. The other end of the rocker arm was attached to a pump that was used to pump water out of mines to keep them from flooding.

Newcomen's pump was better than hand-operated pumps, but was noisy and not very efficient. Several years later, another inventor named James Watt made many improvements to the steam pump. First, he realized

James Watt

POWER OF STEAM

Purpose: To see how steam power works

Materials: aluminum foil, scissors, string, boiling water, oven mitts

Procedure:

1. Cut a circle out of aluminum foil 3 inches in diameter.

2. Starting from the edge, cut in a spiral to the center of the circle and tape a piece of string to the center of the spiral.

3. Heat a pan of water on the stove. When steam begins to rise, use oven mitts to hold the spiral a few inches above the surface of the water. **Be sure** to use the mitts because steam can burn you!

Conclusion: The steam should make the spiral spin or at least move back and forth. In a turbine, steam pushes against the turbine fins or blades and makes it spin. The spinning turbine turns an electromagnet, which in turn generates electrical current.

that the pump would be more efficient if the steam was condensed in a separate chamber from the piston cylinder, so he added a condenser to the pump. Later, he increased the power of the pump by using steam to force the piston in both directions instead of only using it to force the piston up. This was called the double-action pump. These additions greatly improved the steam pump, but still only allowed steam to be used in applications where something was moving up and down.

James Watt added a gear mechanism to the steam pump in 1782, which allowed the up-and-down movement of the piston to be changed into rotational motion. This was the invention of the first steam engine, and Watt received a patent for his ideas. The gear mechanism was called the "sun and planet wheel." The "sun" was a very large gear with a smaller gear attached in the center. The "planet" was another smaller gear that rotated around the center gear, thus turning the "sun" (shown at left). Now the

The sun and planet wheel can be seen on this steam pump.

FUN FACT

What does steam power have to do with popcorn? Popcorn pops because water is stored in a small circle of soft starch in each kernel. As the kernel is heated, the water heats, the droplet of moisture turns to steam, and the steam builds up pressure until the kernel finally explodes to many times its original volume.

pump could be used to move nearly anything with the necessary combination of gears and belts.

The steam engine became useful in many applications. It was used to run rows of looms at a clothing mill, saws in a sawmill, and steam hammers at metal foundries. The Industrial Revolution was well on its way. In 1804 a steam engine was placed on wheels and used as the first locomotive to move cars on a track. And, in 1807, Robert Fulton designed a paddle-wheel boat

Tractor with a steam engine

that was driven by a steam engine. His steamboat made a successful journey on the Hudson river from New York to Albany on August 14, 1807, heralding the beginning of commercial steamboat traffic. Not only did the steam engine revolutionize the factories, but it also revolutionized transportation.

Today, gasoline, diesel, and electric engines have mostly replaced steam engines. However, the power of steam is still used in most power plants. The pressure of expanding steam is used to turn the turbines that generate electricity. Steam is still a vital part of our industrial society. ■

WHAT DID WE LEARN?

- How does steam make things move?
- Who first invented the steam engine?
- How is steam still used in industry today?
- How did Robert Fulton use the steam engine?

TAKING IT FURTHER

- How is a steam engine different from a steam pump?
- Why is the steam engine credited with sparking the Industrial Revolution?

STEAM ENGINE REPORT

Research one industry in which the steam engine made an important difference and either write a report or give an oral report on how the steam engine affected that industry.

TRAIN

Faster than a horse and cart

LESSON 9

Who invented the train?

Words to know:

subway

elevated train

keystone

truss bridge

drawbridge

Challenge words:

magnetic levitation
train/maglev

Have you ever ridden on a train? The invention of the steam engine led to the invention of the train, and the train revolutionized travel. Prior to the invention of the train, all travel was done on foot or in vehicles drawn by animals. But with the invention of the train, man was now able to travel and transport goods quickly from one place to another.

The steam locomotive ruled the rails for over 100 years. The very first steam locomotive was built in 1804 by Richard Trevithick. However, this engine was so heavy it broke the rails and was not successful. Many people began to improve the steam locomotive, and in 1825 an English engineer named George Stephenson built the first successful railway. By 1869 railroad tracks crossed the entire United States from coast to coast and crossed many other countries as well.

A steam locomotive used a fire to heat water into steam. The steam was then used to move a piston, which in turn moved the wheels of the train. Steam locomotives required large amounts of water and coal (or wood) to keep the steam pressure up to power the engine. The ride was sooty and smoky, and frequent stops were required to take on more water, but the train was much faster than a horse and buggy and so it became very popular.

Although steam engines ushered in the train era, by the 1940s most steam engines had been replaced by diesel engines. Diesel engines are more efficient and more powerful than steam engines. The diesel engine was introduced in 1893 by Dr. Rudolph Diesel, and the first reliable diesel engine was produced in 1897. A diesel train does not use a diesel engine to directly drive the train's wheels. Instead, the diesel engine is used to run a generator that generates an electric current. The current runs electric motors that move the wheels. Today, diesel trains are used for transporting goods and people in nearly every part of the world.

Many passenger trains use electricity directly to move the wheels. Electric trains get their energy from overhead wires or from an electrified rail on the ground. Electric trains are quieter and faster than diesel trains and are therefore preferred for passenger travel. The fastest electric train was clocked at 359 mph (578 km/h) in 2007. Most passenger trains travel at speeds much less than this; however, some regularly travel at speeds approaching 150 mph (240 km/h).

When you think of trains, you probably think of a train that travels across the ground; however, many trains travel under the ground. These trains are called subways. The first subway was built in London in 1863. The English often call their subway system "The Tube" because the trains run in underground tunnels or tubes. Many large cities around the world use underground train systems because the trains can take people where they need to go without disrupt-

FUN FACT

The very first trains had crude cars for passengers to ride in, so wealthy people preferred to drive their carriages onto flatbed cars and ride in their carriages. Their horses rode in box cars in another part of the train.

PREPARING FOR A TRAIN

Most trains cannot climb steep hills. Tracks must change direction somewhat slowly and smoothly. Therefore, when laying track across a large area many things must be taken into consideration. If a valley or a mountain lies in the path, either the path must be changed, or a bridge or a tunnel must be built. Often, bridges and tunnels are built to accommodate the train.

The Romans were the master architects of bridges. Many of the arch bridges built during the Roman Empire still stand today. An arch bridge is strong because when force is applied to the keystone, the stone at the top of the arch,

the shape of the arch causes the force to spread outward and downward and thus presses the stones together instead of pushing them apart. Because the arched bridge is so strong, many of the first railroad bridges were arch bridges.

Other railroad bridges are made with trusses. A truss bridge uses a series of triangles to spread out the force. In the picture you can see the series of triangles that make it strong.

Railroad bridges that are built across water must sometimes be designed to lift up to allow boats and ships to pass through. These bridges are called drawbridges.

Suspension bridge

Other railroad bridges are suspension bridges, which use cables to support the weight of the bridge. There is much variety among railroad bridges.

Pretend that you are a railroad bridge engineer. Consider what kind of bridge you would like to build. How much weight will your bridge need to support? What kind of weather conditions must it withstand? Will the bridge be built over water or land? Using soda straws, craft sticks, poster board, and tape, try to build a bridge that is strong enough to hold a toy train.

Arch bridge

Truss bridge

ing the flow of other traffic on the surface. Another type of train that does not run on the ground is the **elevated train**. Elevated trains run on tracks that are built above the ground. This also allows the trains to run without disrupting other traffic.

As with most inventions, the invention of the train led to improvements in other areas as well. Metal rails had to be improved to handle heavier and faster-moving trains. Early rails were made from cast iron. Later rails were made from wrought iron, and today they are made from steel, which is much stronger than iron. Tracks were made by laying rails end to end. This gave the train a clackety-clack sound as the wheels moved over the individual rails. But today's rails, especially for passenger trains, are continuously welded for a much smoother and quieter ride.

Communications also improved as trains became more popular. To keep track of where trains are and to keep them from colliding with each other, good communica-

tion is necessary. Originally, flags were used to pass messages to the train engineers. Telegraph lines were often built alongside the train tracks, so messages could be sent from one control station to another, and the tracks were switched as necessary. Today, computer-controlled dispatchers keep track of each train's location and automatically switch tracks electronically by sending signals to electric motors on the tracks. Train travel is very different today than it was 200 years ago, but it is still a vital part of transportation around the world. ∎

FUN FACT

In 1830 there was a race between a locomotive and a horse to prove that the train was faster. The locomotive, named *Tom Thumb*, broke down during the race so the horse won.

WHAT DID WE LEARN?

- What invention helped spur the invention of the train?
- How long did steam engines dominate the train industry?
- What kinds of trains are common today?
- Why are electric trains preferred for passenger travel?

TAKING IT FURTHER

- Why are diesel trains used more often than electric trains for transporting freight?
- What weather conditions must be considered when building railroad bridges?
- How is a truss bridge similar to an arch bridge?

MAGLEV TRAINS

One of the most recent developments in trains is the **magnetic levitation train**, or **maglev** train. Maglev trains are being developed in several

countries. Electromagnetic coils are used to generate a magnetic field that repels magnets in the body of the train to quickly and smoothly move the train without conventional engines and with no friction. Maglev trains can travel at up to 310 mph (500 km/h).

Currently, Japan and China have working maglev lines, and many other countries are working on technology that may one day make riding the train nearly as fast as flying.

FUN FACT

New York City has the largest underground railway system in the world. It has 842 miles (1,355 km) of track, a small part of which is above ground. The subway system in Moscow, Russia carries the most passengers each year— more than 3 billion.

Transportation

Purpose: To see how magnetic levitation works

Materials: poster board, four block magnets, tape, two nickels

Procedure:

1. Cut two pieces of poster board 2 inches by 6 inches.

2. Lay 3 or more block magnets against one of the pieces with the same pole up as shown in the picture and tape the magnets together.

3. Tape the poster board to the edges of the magnets, thus forming the track.

4. Next, make a train by taping a nickel to each side of a fourth block magnet.

5. Orient the magnet so that the same pole is down as the poles that are up on the magnets on the track. You can test this by seeing if the magnets repel

each other. If they do, you have them in the right orientation.

6. Place your train on the track. The magnets should repel each other and it should be easy to push the train along the track. Keep a loose hold on the train or it will flip over and be pulled down to the other magnets.

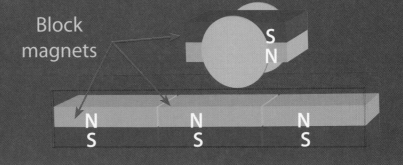

Block magnets

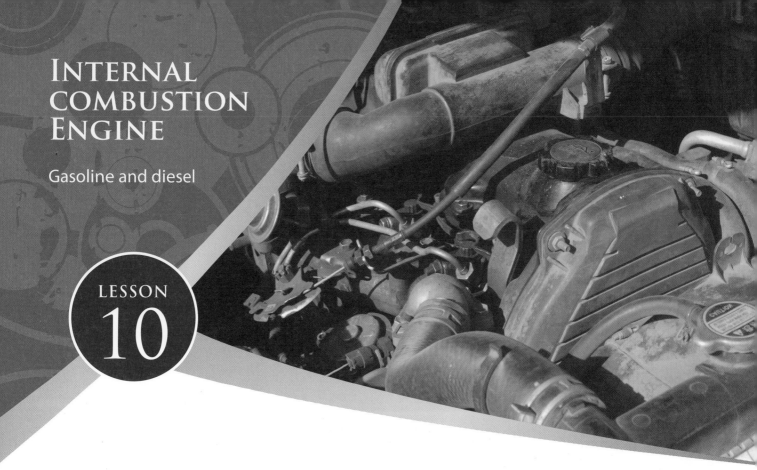

INTERNAL COMBUSTION ENGINE

Gasoline and diesel

LESSON 10

How does a car engine work?

Words to know:

combustion

intake stroke

compression stroke

power stroke

exhaust stroke

Challenge words:

lubricant

Although the development of the steam engine was a monumental boost for the industrial society of the 18th and 19th centuries, it was not a perfect solution for many applications. The steam engine took time to heat the water and build up enough pressure to work. It also required a large amount of fuel to keep the water hot for a long period of time. This was not a problem for a train that could just add a car to carry coal or wood, but a steam engine was not very practical for a personal automobile. Therefore, many people began working on alternative engines. The result was the internal combustion engine.

An internal combustion engine works in a similar way to a steam engine. In a steam engine a piston moves up and down with the expanding volume of steam. In an internal combustion engine a piston moves up and down with the expanding gases from combustion, or explosion, of fuel. The fuel used in a combustion engine can be anything that explodes or burns very rapidly. Many other fuels were tried, but today most internal combustion engines use either gasoline or diesel fuel.

The first working combustion engine was built in 1820 by Reverend W. Cecil. Although Cecil's engine worked, it had some problems, and a French scientist named Etienne Lenoir solved many of these problems. He built the first practical internal combustion engine in 1860. The four-stroke engine, similar to engines that are used today, was designed and built by Gottlieb Daimler in 1889, and the diesel engine was designed and built by Rudolf Diesel in 1892.

Internal combustion engines are used in many applications. Not only are they used in cars, trucks, and other automobiles, but they are also used in lawn mowers, boats, motorcycles, and chain saws.

The four-stroke engine is the design used in most gasoline engines today. Shown here is a diagram of a cylinder in an internal combustion engine. During the first stroke, called the intake stroke, the intake valve opens and fuel mixed with air enters the cylinder as the piston moves down. During the second stroke, the piston moves up and compresses the gas. This is called the compression stroke. At the top of the compression stroke a spark from the spark plug ignites the fuel causing an explosion, which pushes the piston down. This is the third stroke, called the power stroke. The fourth stroke, the exhaust stroke, occurs as the piston rises again and pushes the remaining gases out the exhaust valve.

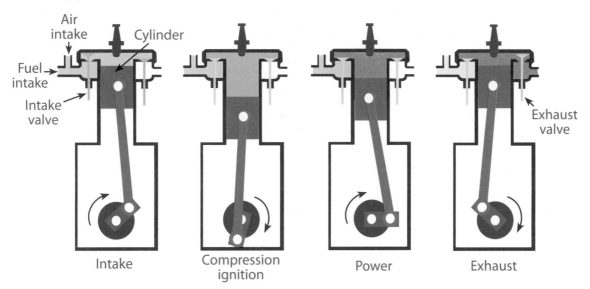

Air intake
Fuel intake
Intake valve
Cylinder
Exhaust valve

Intake   Compression ignition   Power   Exhaust

These four strokes occur over and over again, many times each minute. Most automobile engines have four to eight cylinders. Each cylinder is set up to fire at a slightly different time so that there is continuous power applied to the wheels of the car. In order to keep the power constant, the timing of the movement of the pistons is critical. Also, the timing for the firing of the spark plugs is very important. The spark needs to occur at just the right time to get maximum power from the explosion. This timing is controlled by computers in most newer vehicles.

A diesel engine works somewhat differently from a gasoline engine. A diesel engine does not have an ignition system—that is, it does not have any spark plugs. Instead, during the intake stroke only air is brought into the cylinder. As the air is compressed during the compression stroke it heats up. At the height of the

INTERNAL COMBUSTION ENGINE

Copy each pattern piece from the "Internal Combustion Engine Pattern" handout onto poster board or tag board. Cut out each piece and assemble them together as described on the pattern sheet. This gives you a model of a cylinder and piston. If you like, you can make four cylinders and place them side by side to represent a car engine. Review what is occurring during each stroke of the piston by moving the parts to match the pictures above demonstrating the intake, compression, power, and exhaust strokes.

Oil refineries like this one turn crude oil into gasoline and diesel fuel.

compression stroke, diesel fuel is sprayed into the cylinder and the heat from the compressed air causes the fuel to ignite. This causes the power stroke, just as the explosion in the gasoline engine does. A diesel engine is more efficient than a gasoline engine. It produces more force to move the vehicle per gallon of fuel. However, the engine must be heavier to accommodate the additional pressure built up inside the cylinders as well as the additional heat produced during the compression. Therefore, diesel engines are not practical for all applications. ■

WHAT DID WE LEARN?

- What is an internal combustion engine?
- What are the main fuels used in combustion engines today?
- What are the four stages or functions of the four-stroke engine?

TAKING IT FURTHER

- How does the movement of a piston turn a car's wheels?
- How is the action of an engine similar to the action of riding a bicycle?

COOLING AN ENGINE

An internal combustion engine produces great pressure and large amounts of heat. To withstand the pressure created inside the cylinders, the engine block must be made of very thick metal.

Heat is produced inside an engine in two ways. First, compression of gases and the explosion of the fuel produce heat. Second, the movement between the piston and the cylinder produces friction, which in turn produces heat.

In order to keep the metal parts from melting, much of this heat must be removed from the engine. First, to reduce friction, all of the moving parts inside the engine are coated with a **lubricant** such as engine oil. Lubricants allow the parts to move more freely without generating as much heat.

The second way heat is removed from the engine is by a cooling system. Smaller engines, such as lawn mower or motorcycle engines, transmit heat directly into the air. These engines usually have fins over which the air moves. The heat from the engine moves into the air and is carried away. Larger engines, such as those in cars and trucks, need more than the movement of air to remove heat. Most vehicles have a water-cooling system. Water is stored in a radiator. During operation, water is pumped from the radiator through tubes around the engine block. Heat moves from the engine into the water. The

water then returns to the radiator where the heat moves into the air around the radiator. The cooled water is then sent back to the engine block to remove more heat.

Purpose: To understand how cooling systems work

Materials: six metal bolts, saucepan, three cereal bowls, "Cooling an Engine" worksheet

Procedure:

1. Place six metal bolts into a small saucepan with 1 cup of water.

2. Heat the water on the stove until it is boiling. This will heat up the bolts just like an engine heats up.

3. Using a spoon, carefully remove the bolts from the water and place two bolts in each of three cereal bowls.

4. Pour ½ cup cold water into the first bowl; blow gently on the bolts in the second bowl for one minute; do nothing with the bolts in the third bowl.

5. Measure the temperature of the water in each cup and record your findings on a copy of "Cooling an Engine" worksheet.

6. Pour out the water from the first bowl and touch each of the bolts and compare the temperature of the bolts in each bowl. (Some of the bolts may still be hot, so be careful.) Record your observations on your worksheet and answer the questions on the worksheet.

AUTOMOBILE

Dad, can I borrow the car?

LESSON

11

Who invented the automobile?

Words to know:

alternative fuels

In 1250 Sir Roger Bacon said, "One day it will be possible to build vehicles, which will move of their own accord and no longer have to be drawn by horses or other animals." It would be over 500 years before this prediction would come true. The great scientist and artist Leonardo da Vinci designed many mechanical vehicles from 1482 to 1499; however, he lacked an engine with which to power these vehicles. It wasn't until 1782, when James Watt made the first practical steam engine, that man began to see the fulfillment of Bacon's and da Vinci's ideas. In 1784 Watt applied for a patent for a steam-driven carriage which he called a horseless coach, but he never completed his plan. In 1801, Richard Trevithick built what is recognized as the first steam-driven carriage.

Steam-powered automobiles were slow to catch on because they were not very practical. As we mentioned in the previous lesson, steam engines take time to heat the water into steam, and they require a large amount of fuel in order to travel a long distance. So automobiles did not really become popular until Gottlieb Daimler invented the 4-stroke internal combustion engine in 1889. Daimler and Carl Benz are considered the fathers of the German automobile industry. The history of the automobile from 1900 on is filled with names you probably recognize; names like Rolls, Renault, Chrysler, Chevrolet, and of course, Ford.

First affordable car

Henry Ford did not invent the automobile, but he made the automobile affordable for the average person. Ford started his first automobile factory in 1903 with the goal of building a reliable, low-cost vehicle. His first Model-T was produced in 1908 and sold for $950. This was still a lot of money in 1908 so Ford worked to bring the price down. He designed the assembly line and insisted that the parts for the cars would be interchangeable so that they could be mass produced. This greatly reduced the price of the Model-T and at one time the cars sold for as little as $280. Model-Ts were produced for 19 years and over 15 million of them were sold in the United States alone. This was the beginning of the automobile for the common man.

Later improvements

Although the internal combustion engine was the major invention needed to usher in the age of the automobile, many other inventions were needed to make the automobile what it is today. Mechanical engineers improved the suspension systems, steering mechanisms, transmissions, and wheels. Charles Goodyear invented a vulcanization process to make rubber for tires that would not melt in the summer heat. Other engineers improved the ignition system. And in today's cars, computer controls play a vital part.

Model-T

When designing an automobile, the engineers must take many factors into consideration. They must first consider function. What is this vehicle going to be used for? Is it a family car, a farm truck, a school bus, or a military tank? Depending on its function, the vehicle will be designed differently for safety, cost, fuel efficiency, engine power, and comfort. A family car must be safe, affordable, get reasonable gas mileage, and be reasonably comfortable. A luxury car will cost more and have more comforts and gadgets. A military tank will be designed very differently from a family car.

Alternative fuel vehicles

Although most automobiles today use gasoline or diesel fuel to power their engines, there are some newer vehicles that use alternative fuels. Gasoline and diesel fuel both come from petroleum, which

DESIGN A CAR

Use your imagination to design your dream car. What would you use it for? What would it look like? What features would it have? What kind of fuel would it use? Draw pictures of your vehicle and explain how it works and how it is different from cars that are available today.

is an oily substance that is found underground. It is believed that there is a limited amount of petroleum, so many people are working to design practical vehicles that do not use petroleum. One alternative is to use biodiesel fuel—a fuel that is made from vegetable oil, such as soybean oil. Corn is also being processed into ethanol, another fuel alternative.

Two of the most promising new types of automobiles are electric vehicles and hydrogen vehicles. Electric vehicles use batteries to drive electric motors that turn the wheels of the car. Electric vehicles are very quiet and produce less pollution than traditional internal combustion vehicles. However, electric vehicles have some problems. The batteries cannot power a vehicle for long trips without recharging every few hours. This creates a problem if you want to drive across the country. Also, electric vehicles are more expensive and less available than gasoline cars. Scientists and engineers are working on these problems.

Another promising alternative to gasoline-powered engines is hydrogen. Hydrogen vehicles burn hydrogen gas. Some vehicles have a combustion engine that is powered by hydrogen; others use hydrogen fuel cells. Hydrogen fuel cells take hydrogen and oxygen and chemically combine them together to produce water and electricity. The electricity can then be used to power the vehicle. Hydrogen vehicles have some difficulties as well. For example, hydrogen is not readily available like gasoline. Also, the cost of hydrogen vehicles is higher than the cost of gasoline vehicles. But in time, hydrogen vehicles are likely to become more popular as these problems are solved. ■

WHAT DID WE LEARN?

- Why were internal combustion engines better than steam engines for automobiles?

- What are some alternative fuel sources to gasoline and diesel fuel?

- What are some parts of the automobile that have been improved over the years?

- What was Henry Ford's major contribution to the automobile industry?

TAKING IT FURTHER

- What kinds of vehicles use internal combustion engines other than cars and trucks?

- What factors must be considered when designing an automobile?

- What other industries have benefited from the automobile industry?

ALTERNATIVE FUELS

Research alternative-fuel vehicles. Some vehicles that are available today are hybrid cars. This means that they have two power sources. For example, the vehicle may have an internal combustion engine and electric batteries. The car may use the batteries most of the time and use the combustion engine to boost power or charge the batteries when they get low. See what you can find out about hybrid cars or other alternative fuels and write 1–2 pages about what you learn.

JET ENGINE

Moving air

LESSON 12

How does a jet engine work?

Words to know:

thrust

turbine

Challenge words:

Newton's third law of motion

Boyle's law

Have you ever been on a big jet-powered airplane? If you have, you know the thrill of zooming down the runway faster and faster until you finally lift into the air. There is a whole industry and a multitude of inventions that make this experience possible. One of the most important inventions contributing to today's airline industry is the development of the jet engine.

With the invention of the steam engine, inventors tried to use it for nearly every application. The steam engine was very successful with trains and had limited success with cars. It was even tried in aircraft in 1874, and again in 1890. But the steam engine was just too heavy for use in aircraft. The first airplane to successfully fly was developed by

Heinkel HE 178, the first jet airplane

the Wright brothers in 1903, using a gasoline-powered internal combustion engine. Since that time, airplanes and airplane engines have continuously been improved. The first gasoline jet engine was developed by Frank Whittle in England in the 1930s. And the first jet airplane was the Heinkel HE 178, invented by the Germans in 1939, and used in World War II.

The idea behind a jet engine is very simple. Essentially, a jet engine is a hollow tube where air enters at one end and is forced out the back at a greater speed and force than it entered. This creates thrust. **Thrust** is the power needed to move the aircraft forward. Although this simple design was adequate for early aircraft, this very simple engine does not create the forces needed for modern aircraft. So the simple jet engine has been modified into the turbo jet engine.

A turbo jet has three main parts. The first or forward part of the engine is called the compressor. The compressor contains a series of blades that spin and draw air into the engine while compressing the air. The air can be compressed up to 40 times its original volume. When the air is compressed, the temperature rises. Thus, the air exiting the compressor is very dense and very hot.

After the air passes through the compressor, it enters the combustion chamber. Here the superheated air is mixed with some kind of fuel. This fuel is usually jet fuel, but can also be kerosene, propane, or other fuel. The fuel is sprayed in by a fuel injection system. When the fuel is mixed with the superheated air, it burns very quickly. The exhaust gases from the burning fuel exit the back of the engine at tremendous speed, thus resulting in a large amount of thrust.

At the back of the engine is a turbine. The **turbine** is a series of blades that turn when the exhaust gases push against them. In an airplane engine, the turbine is connected to the compressor by a shaft, so the air that recently passed through the compressor is used to move the compressor to draw in more air, and the exhaust gases exiting the turbine create the thrust needed to move the aircraft forward.

> ## FUN FACT
>
> The world's fastest jet-powered aircraft is the SR-71 Blackbird. It's official speed record is about Mach 3.3, or 3.3 times the speed of sound—about 2,500 mph (4,040 km/h).

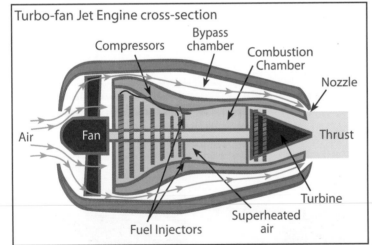

Turbo-fan Jet Engine cross-section

Compressors · Bypass chamber · Combustion Chamber · Nozzle · Air · Fan · Thrust · Turbine · Superheated air · Fuel Injectors

JET ENGINES

Complete the "Jet Engine" worksheet to help you better understand the parts and function of a turbo-fan jet engine.

In small aircraft, the jet engine may be a turbo-prop engine. In a turbo-prop, the turbine is connected to a propeller instead of to a compressor. However, large commercial planes have turbo-fan engines. A turbo-fan engine has a large fan in front of the compressor to help draw in the air. The fan draws in much more air than the compressor can handle. Much of the air is forced around the compressor and out the back, like a simple jet engine. This provides much of the thrust needed for take off. The rest of the air is forced through the compressor where it is combined with fuel and used to move the turbines. The turbo-fan engine is much quieter than a regular turbo jet engine and is more fuel efficient as well.

Jet engines can be used for more than just airplanes. If the turbine is connected to a shaft instead of to the compressor it is called a turbo-shaft engine. This shaft can be connected to the blades of a helicopter or the treads of a tank. Some turbo-shaft engines are even used in power plants. In many power plants, steam is used to move turbines that in turn generate electricity. But in some power plants, jet engines are used to move the turbines to generate electricity. ■

WHAT DID WE LEARN?

- How does a simple jet engine work?
- What are the three main parts of a turbo jet engine?
- What is the purpose of jet fuel in a turbo jet engine?
- In what applications are jet engines used, other than for airplanes?

TAKING IT FURTHER

- Why were steam engines abandoned as possible airplane engines?
- Why are jet engines not used in most cars and trucks?
- How is a jet engine power plant similar to a coal power plant? How are they different?
- How does a turbo-fan engine create more thrust than the straight turbo jet engine?

BOYLE'S LAW

Turbo jet engines operate on two scientific principles. The first principle is **Newton's third law of motion**, which states that for every action there is an equal and opposite reaction. The second principle affecting turbo jet engines is called **Boyle's law**. Boyle's law shows that when a gas is compressed, its volume decreases proportionally to the pressure applied and its temperature increases proportionally to the pressure applied. Explain how each of these principles applies to the turbo jet engine by completing the "Boyle's Law" worksheet.

AIRPLANE

I can fly!

Who invented the airplane and how does it fly?

Words to know:

Bernoulli's principle

airfoil

lift

weight

thrust

drag

pitch

roll

yaw

For hundreds, perhaps thousands, of years man has dreamed of flying. His first successful attempt involved a hot air balloon, which allowed him to rise above the earth and travel through the air. However, the hot air balloon was very limited in how high it could go and it was very difficult to control where it went. Something better was bound to be invented. Many different ideas were tried. Some were reasonable, and some bordered on ridiculous.

The first airplane

The first successful airplane flight was December 17, 1903, at Kittyhawk, North Carolina. Wilbur and Orville Wright made history by flying the first motorized airplane. After this first flight, flying was slow to catch on in America, but was an instant hit in Europe. Flying soon became accepted in America as well, and by World War I, airplanes were an integral part of the military.

The years between World War I and World War II are considered the Golden Age of Aviation. There was a constant stream of new inventions and new records set by flyers and their planes. In 1927 Charles Lindbergh flew the first solo non-stop flight across the Atlantic Ocean, flying from New York City to Paris. The world was in love with aviators and airplanes.

Advancements

Since World War II, airplanes have continued to advance in many ways. Today we have planes that are highly specialized. The different jets used by the military are designed for bombing, air combat, troop transport, or reconnaissance. Some aircraft have been specially designed for stealth operations and are virtually undetectable by enemy radar. Nonmilitary aircraft have been designed for passenger travel or freight hauling. Some planes are specifically designed for scientific purposes such as weather monitoring or speed testing. Whatever the purpose, airplanes are now an integral part of life.

In addition to aircraft design, aviation has led to advances in many related areas. For example, radar technology was developed for the military, but has found many civilian uses as well. Computer technology has advanced hand in hand with aviation. Navigation systems have been developed, which have benefited aviation and many other industries as well. Finally, weapons systems have been developed to take advantage of the advances in aircraft design.

Scientific principles

Regardless of the style or use of the airplane, all aircraft operate under the same scientific principles. **Bernoulli's principle** states that as a fluid (or air) increases in velocity it decreases in pressure. With respect to an airplane, this means that as air goes faster it exerts less pressure. This is the fundamental reason that airplanes can fly. The cross section of the wing of an airplane is shaped like the **airfoil** shown here. The

surface of the top of the wing is longer than the surface of the bottom of the wing, so air must flow faster over the top than it does under the wing. This causes the air pressure to be less above the wing than it is below the wing. As

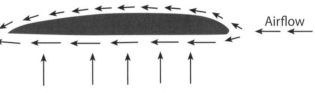
Airflow

the airplane moves faster, the difference in air pressure becomes greater. When the upward pressure below the wing is greater than the weight of the airplane, the plane lifts off of the ground. Appropriately, this force is called lift, and it is the first of four forces we are going to examine.

In addition to lift, there are three other forces affecting the behavior of the airplane. **Lift** is the force acting in an upward direction on the plane. The force acting in the opposite direction is the **weight** of the plane as it is pulled down by gravity. Lift must be greater than weight in order for the plane to fly. The third force is **thrust**. This is the forward force produced by the engines. The thrust must be sufficient for the plane to move fast enough to create lift. Finally, since the plane is flying through air and not through a vacuum, it is constantly being bombarded by air molecules. These molecules push against the plane as it moves forward. This force is called **drag**. Drag slows the airplane down. These four forces—lift, weight, thrust, and drag—must all balance out in order for a plane to fly.

AIRPLANE MOVEMENTS

Complete the "Airplane Movements" worksheet to better understand the forces and movements of airplanes.

A 747 jumbo jet

Types of movement

Once the plane is in the air, it can move in three dimensions. A vehicle on the ground can move in only two dimensions. It can move forward or backward, and it can move from side to side. But an airplane can move in three dimensions. An airplane can move up or down in the air as it goes forward. This movement is called pitch. A plane can also tip side to side as one of the wings dips lower than the other. This movement is called roll. Finally, an airplane can turn right or left and this is called yaw. A pilot quickly learns to think of his/her plane's movement in terms of pitch, roll, and yaw.

When you consider the advancements made in aviation in the past 100 years it is mind boggling, and it is nearly impossible to imagine what air vehicles will be like in another hundred years. But whatever changes come are sure to be exciting. ■

WHAT DID WE LEARN?

- Explain each of the four forces that affect airplane flight.
- Explain how Bernoulli's principle causes lift.
- Explain the three different ways that a plane moves in the air.

TAKING IT FURTHER

- How is Newton's third law of motion applied to airplanes?
- What will happen to an airplane if the power is reduced in the engine?

PAPER AIRPLANES

Take what you have learned about lift, thrust, weight, and drag, and experiment with different designs of paper airplanes. Use different weights of paper with the same design to see the effect of weight. Make planes with different shapes and sizes to test the effects of drag and lift. And finally, give different amounts of force when flying the same plane several times to see the effects of thrust. Every person's designs will be slightly different so his/her results will be different, but it will be fun to guess how a plane will fly, and then to test it. If you need help in designing a paper airplane, there are many web sites or library books that will give you patterns and ideas.

Orville Wright   Wilbur Wright

THE WRIGHT BROTHERS

Two brothers, two friends, two of a minister's five children—these two brothers, neither of whom finished high school or had any formal training in science, did what man had dreamed of for hundreds of years. Orville and Wilbur Wright were the first two men to have controlled flight using man-made power.

Wilbur, the older of the two, was born on April 16, 1867, and Orville came along four years later on August 19, 1871. They were close right from the start. Wilbur once said that, "From the time we were children, my brother Orville and myself lived together, played together, worked together and, in fact, thought together." They were about as close as two brothers could be.

They had always had a way with tools and were able to solve difficult problems. Their niece, Ivonette, once recalled how when her toys were broken her two uncles would fix them better than they had been to begin with.

The two men never married, and they lived with their father along with their unmarried sister. They felt their mechanical ability came from their mother, who died in 1889 from tuberculosis. Their father gave them something else that was very important—strong encouragement. He was a man of iron will and absolute self-confidence. He instilled in them the belief that with hard work and determination they could accomplish anything they set out to do.

Wilbur and Orville were always tinkering. Orville built kites that he sold to his classmates. He later developed an enthusiasm for printing. After using a toy press for a while, he built a press out of parts from a junk yard. Later, while in junior high, he designed and built a larger press out of scrap parts and firewood. Orville dropped out of school and opened his own print shop. He started a weekly paper in Dayton, Ohio, where they were living. Wilbur joined the company and a year later they decided to publish a daily paper, but were unable to compete against the big papers. They decided to change their business to printing cards, posters, and other items.

When the bicycle craze hit the country, the brothers bought bikes and became cyclists. Wilbur liked long rides in the country, while Orville went into racing. Their friends would bring their bikes around for repairs and the Wrights' reputation as skilled mechanics spread. In 1892 they put their friend Ed Sines in charge of the printing business, and opened the Wright Cycle Company where they sold, rented, repaired, and later manufactured bicycles.

During the 1890s many men were working

on different machines in hopes of producing controlled flight. One of them was a German named Otto Lilienthal, who made almost two thousand flights in his gliders before an accident in one of them took his life in 1896. Stories of his flights and death were printed in papers all around the world. These stories aroused the Wrights' interest in flying, and they both started reading all they could find about flight. They found that a practical flying machine needed three things: wings to lift it, power to propel it, and a way to control it. Many people had worked on the first two requirements, but almost no work had been done on control. So the brothers got to work.

They spent a few years studying and trying out designs using kites, which were not what you might think of as a kite, but rather more like gliders with strings. By 1900 they felt they needed to try out their control system on a full-sized man-carrying glider, and to do this they needed a place that had strong steady winds. With the help of the U.S. Weather Bureau, they found a remote location in North Carolina's outer banks called Kitty Hawk. Once there, they spent about three weeks testing the glider unmanned, taking measurements, and making changes. Finally, they felt it was ready. Wilbur was the pilot and in one day he made 12 flights. This showed that their control system worked.

That winter they made a bigger glider using calculations from Otto Lilienthal's work, and returned to Kitty Hawk in 1901. This year was disappointing to the brothers. The flyer did not have the lift they hoped for, and the controls did not work well. So they went home and built a wind tunnel to test different wing shapes. Using the results from their own testing, they were able to generate the charts and numbers they needed to design a better flyer.

The next year their work paid off. They made hundreds of test flights with both broth-ers taking turns flying the glider. They were able to work out the last few problems with their controls, and proved the accuracy of their lab tests.

Now they were ready to fly using power. They contacted several engine manufacturers, asking if they could make a motor with at least 8 horsepower that weighed less then 200 pounds. None of the manufacturers would even try. So the brothers decided to build their own engine, making many of the parts in their bike shop. Their new engine weighed 179 pounds and was able to generate more then 12 horsepower.

Once the engine was completed, they then had to figure out how to build the propeller. Through studies and experiments, and five notebooks filled with data, they were able to come up with a design. Orville said to a friend, "Isn't it astonishing that all these secrets have been preserved for so many years just so that we could discover them! Well, our propellers are so different from any that have been used before that they will have to either be a good deal better or a good deal worse."

In 1903 they went back to Kitty Hawk to try a powered flight. The first day they had a small mishap when the wind caught the flyer and slightly damaged it. After making repairs, they were successful on December 17. They made four flights that day with witnesses to prove it could be done. They spent the next two years perfecting their flyer so they could turn and make circles. They then decided to ground themselves until they got the patents through. Orville spent time selling the airplane to the U.S. army, while Wilbur went to France to sell their plane there. They were both heroes to the world.

Wilbur came down with typhoid fever and died in 1912, while his brother Orville lived to see their simple design developed into a jet. He died in January 1948.

ROCKET ENGINE

Reaching for space

LESSON 14

How does a rocket work?

Words to know:

propellant

oxidizer

cryogenic fuels

hypergolic fuels

Challenge words:

V-2 rocket

The Wright brothers reached for the sky and made it; however, others had higher aspirations. Science fiction writers had been writing about space travel for many years, but it wasn't until the early twentieth century that scientists began to think there was a real possibility that man could someday travel into space. However, before man could reach into space, he needed a way to break free of earth's gravitational pull. The rocket engine was the answer; but rockets had to go through many developments before they were ready to reach into space.

Early rockets

Early rockets were used primarily for military use. The Chinese have been using rockets since the 1200s, mainly as explosive weapons. Scientists first began to understand the principles behind rockets in the 1600s when Sir Isaac Newton published his laws of motion, and by the 1800s Europeans were using rockets as military weapons as well. But these rockets were not ready for space travel.

Robert H. Goddard began experimenting with rockets in the early 1900s, and in 1919 he wrote a book on rocket flight called *A Method of Reaching Extreme Altitudes*. Goddard performed the first flight of a liquid-fueled rocket on March 16, 1926. He continued his work on rockets and flew the first rocket to

Robert H. Goddard's first rocket at the launch site

go faster than the speed of sound in 1935. Today, Robert Goddard is considered the father of modern rocketry; however, during his lifetime people did not take his work seriously. It wasn't until after rockets were used during World War II that the idea of sending rockets into space took hold.

After World War II, Werner Von Braun and other German scientists came to America to help develop rockets, and Soviet scientists began working on rockets in earnest as well. The earliest rockets were unreliable, but as rockets became more reliable, a race began to see who would be the first nation to get to space. The Soviet Union was the first to launch a satellite into space, followed a few weeks later by the United States. Today, many nations have rockets that can reach into space.

Newton's third law of motion states that for every action there is an equal and opposite reaction. This is the main physical law describing the way rockets work. A rocket shoots up because hot gases shoot down out of the bottom of the rocket engine. The hot gases are produced as the propellant is burned and then directed through a nozzle out the back of the engine. The propellant is a combination of rocket fuel and an oxidizer.

Kinds of propellants

There are three basic kinds of rocket propellants. One type is solid and the other two are liquid. Solid rocket fuel contains both the fuel and the oxidizer in a powdered form mixed with a binder to form a solid material. Solid fuel is always ready to use and just needs to be ignited. Older rockets used a fuse to light the propellant, but most solid rocket fuel today is ignited by an electrical charge. Solid rocket fuel is stable and easy to store, but is not ideal for all situations. For one thing, once a solid rocket engine is ignited, it cannot be shut off. It will burn until all of the fuel is spent. This is fine for initial launch, but does not help if the rocket needs to change course after the fuel is used up. Also, solid rocket engines have more thrust the more fuel they have. So the initial thrust is great, but the thrust decreases as the fuel is used up, and there is no way to control the amount of thrust once the engine is ignited.

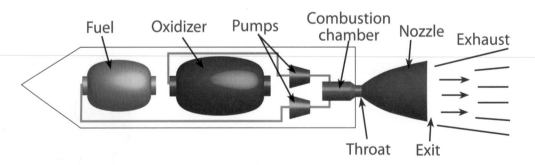

Liquid-fuel rocket engines solve some of these problems, yet have challenges of their own. The most common type of liquid fuel rocket engine uses cryogenic fuel. Cryogenic means very cold. Cryogenic fuels are fuels that normally occur as a gas, but as they are cooled and placed under great pressure, they become liquid. The most common cryogenic liquid fuel is hydrogen. Many rockets use liquid hydrogen as the fuel and liquid oxygen as the oxidizer. This type of rocket engine is more complex than a solid fuel rocket engine. It requires a series of pumps and gauges to regulate the flow of the propellants. Also, it is more difficult to store liquid fuels because they must be kept at such a cold temperature and under pressure. However, liquid fuel rocket engines can be turned on and off and can control the thrust by controlling the flow of the propellants. Also, because hydrogen and oxygen combine to produce water, they do not produce the pollutants that other fuels produce.

The third kind of rocket engine uses **hypergolic fuels**. Hypergolic is a big sounding word that means that two substances ignite when they come in contact with each other. This kind of engine does not require an ignition system like the other types of rockets. However, the substances used can be somewhat unstable and can produce toxic pollutants as a result of the chemical reaction. Only a few types of rockets use hypergolic fuels.

Transportation

TESTING ROCKETS

We don't want you to ruin your home, so we are not going to have you test real rockets in your living room. However, we can do some fun tests to learn a little more about rockets using a balloon. A balloon demonstrates Newton's third law of motion.

Purpose: To demonstrate how a rocket works

Materials: balloon, tag board, tape, soda straw, string

Activity 1—Procedure:

1. Blow up a balloon and let it go. Watch it fly forward as the air rushes out the back of the balloon. What kind of path did the balloon take? It probably flew in a very erratic path.

When scientists first began building rockets, they had trouble getting them to go where they wanted them to go. So, one of the first things that scientists added to the rocket was stabilizing fins.

Activity 2—Procedure:

1. Cut three or four fins from tag board.

2. Fill your balloon again and tape your tag board fins around the edge of your balloon to make fins for your balloon rocket.

3. Release the balloon and see how the fins affect the flight. Did it fly straighter?

Another important addition to rockets in the more recent past was a guidance system. You can add a guidance system to your rocket as well.

Activity 3—Procedure:

1. Tape a soda straw lengthwise to the side of your balloon.

2. Thread a string through the straw.

3. Tape one end of the string to one side of the room.

4. Blow up the balloon and hold the end shut.

5. Tape the other end of the string to the other side of the room.

6. Pull the balloon to the end of the string and let it go. How did its path compare to the first flight?

It probably had a much straighter path because the string made corrections to the flight path in the same way that computers can use thrusters to correct the space shuttle's path.

Design considerations

All rocket designers must consider two main factors when designing a rocket engine. First, they must consider weight. The engine must provide enough thrust to not only lift the rocket and its payload, passengers, and instruments, but it must also lift all of the rocket fuel. In general, the total weight of a rocket on the launch pad is about 91% propellant, 3% tanks and engine, and 6% payload, people, and instrumentation. This means that about 94% of the thrust is used to lift the weight of the rocket engine and fuel. The second consideration is the type of fuel needed. If the rocket engine is lifting something that is going to be traveling around in space, it will need to use liquid fuel that can be computer controlled. If the rocket is only going to one location, a solid-fuel engine may be sufficient. For example, a rocket carrying a bomb may use a solid-fuel rocket engine. But a space probe may be powered by a liquid-fueled rocket. The space shuttle actually uses a liquid-fueled engine with solid rocket boosters, which add thrust during take off. ■

WHAT DID WE LEARN?

- Who first explained the scientific principles behind rockets?

- What is the third law of motion?

- Who is considered the father of modern rocketry?

- What is a propellant?

- What are the three types of rocket fuel used today?

TAKING IT FURTHER

- What are two important things that an engineer must consider when designing a rocket engine?

- Why do you think model rocket engines are made from solid rocket fuel?

- Many rockets burn their fuel in two or three stages. Why might they be designed this way?

- How can a rocket engine work in space where there is no air?

- Would you expect a rocket engine to be more or less efficient in space? Why?

V-2 ROCKET

One of the most important and most dangerous rockets invented in the twentieth century was the German **V-2 rocket**. The German army developed this rocket and used it to bomb London. Research the V-2 rocket project and write a summary of what you learned about it.

SPACECRAFT

Escaping from earth

LESSON 15

What types of spacecraft help us explore space?

Words to know:

satellite

space probe

In 1903 Konstantian Tsiolkovksy, a Russian scientist, worked on a theory of space flight. He built a wind tunnel and tested the effects of rapid movement through air. From these tests he calculated the speed needed to escape earth's atmosphere. He knew that a rocket would be needed to provide the required speed. However, the necessary rocket was not invented until 1949, when Werner Von Braun launched a rocket 240 miles into space.

Much of what Von Braun learned about rockets came from his work on the German V-2 rocket; however, Von Braun was committed to building rockets for space travel not war. After World War II, many of the scientists that worked on wartime rockets turned their attention to peacetime uses of rockets. Many of those scientists came to the United States and many others went to the Soviet Union. The Soviet Union put the first satellite, *Sputnik*, into space in 1957 and actually sent the first rocket to the moon in September 1959. The rocket crashed on the moon and the instruments were unable to communicate with earth, but scientists showed that rockets could reach far into space. At the same time the United States was also working on its space program, and in 1969 they sent the first men to the moon.

Since that time rockets have been used to send a variety of objects and people into space. Satellites are some of the most important things placed in space by rockets. Satellites are anything that orbits the earth. Many satellites are used for communication purposes such as cellular phones, long distance phone calls, and television signals. Other satellites track weather systems. One of the most interesting satellites is the Hubble Space Telescope, which is used to view space from a position above the atmosphere for clear viewing of the far reaches of space.

Billows of steam rise as the space shuttle begins to lift off.

Rockets are also used to launch space probes. Space probes have been sent to explore every planet in our solar system. Probes have also been sent to explore comets, moons, and asteroids. One of the most interesting probes in recent history is the *Cassini-Huygens* space probe. This probe was launched on June 30, 2004. It was sent to Saturn on a four-year mission to study the ringed planet and its moons. *Cassini-Huygens* is really two probes in one. *Cassini* is the main spacecraft and *Huygens* is a smaller probe that was deployed in January 2005 to Titan, Saturn's largest moon.

Cassini contains equipment for measuring magnetic fields, and radar and photo equipment for taking pictures in the visible, ultraviolet, and infrared spectrums. Many probes have solar panels for power, but Saturn is too far from the sun for solar panels to be effective; therefore, *Cassini* has a nuclear power supply. *Cassini* also contains two large rocket engines for propulsion as well at 16 smaller jet thrusters for making minor course changes.

In addition to satellites and space probes, rockets have been used to launch several space stations into orbit around the earth. Early space stations included Skylab and Mir. The current space station is the International Space Station which is a joint project between six different space agencies and over ten nations. The International Space Station has been continually occupied since November 2, 2000. This is an orbiting laboratory where a variety of experiments are conducted in near zero gravity.

One of the most spectacular displays of rocketry is the launching of the space shuttle. The large liquid-fueled rocket engine burns approximately 47,000 gallons (178,000 liters) of liquid hydrogen and 17,000 gallons (64,000 liters) of liquid oxygen per minute during lift off. This engine is so efficient that nearly 99% of the fuel provides power. In addition, two solid rocket boosters are connected to the sides of the shuttle to provide additional thrust.

In the future, rockets will continue to be used to launch various kinds of spacecraft into space. NASA currently has plans to design and build a generation of reus-

SPACECRAFT OF THE FUTURE

Design your own spacecraft. Decide on its purpose. Is it a satellite, a probe, or will it carry people? What will it be used for? Will it be reused? Will it need to move through an atmosphere or only in space? Draw a picture of your spacecraft and write a short description of how it will be used and the special features it will have.

able craft that will take men to the moon where a more permanent base will be built. Long term, people want to reach other planets. Mars is the most likely planet for man to visit in the future.

Although much of the work done by NASA and other space agencies has been done with the goal of showing how life began, as Christians we don't need to spend billions of dollars and travel to far reaches of the universe to understand where life came from. We only need to read Genesis chapter 1 and recognize the glory of the universe created by God. ■

WHAT DID WE LEARN?

- What is a spacecraft?
- List three different kinds of spacecraft?
- What two countries have led the way in the development of spacecraft?
- What scientist launched the first rocket into space?
- What is the Cassini-Huygens probe?

TAKING IT FURTHER

- Why does the Huygens space probe need a heat shield?
- Why does Cassini use a nuclear power source instead of solar panels?
- What is one advantage to a space telescope such as Hubble?

SPACE STATION FACTS

Visit NASA's web site (www.nasa.gov/mission_pages/station/main/index.html) and read more about the International Space Station. Then fill in the facts on the "International Space Station Facts" worksheet.

The International Space Station as seen from the Space Shuttle *Endeavour*

HOVERCRAFT

Floating on air

LESSON 16

What is a hovercraft and how does it hover?

Words to know:

hovercraft

vectored thrust system

Challenge words:

hydrofoil

One of the biggest barriers to efficient travel is friction. When two surfaces rub against each other, frictional forces resist the movement. Many vehicles use wheels to help reduce friction. But a relatively new invention takes a different approach. **Hovercraft** are designed to travel over a cushion of air, thus limiting the amount of friction. This makes hovercraft very efficient.

Hovercraft, also called ACVs, or air-cushioned vehicles, can travel over land or water because they do not actually touch the surface when they are moving. Most hovercraft are shaped somewhat like a boat. But instead of having a hull, the edge of the craft is surrounded by a flexible rubber skirt. This skirt traps air that is pumped under the craft by large fans called turbines. The trapped air becomes compressed thus raising the air pressure under the craft and lifting it above the surface. Large fans or propellers at the rear of the craft push air backwards, which results in forward movement of the hovercraft. This movement is very smooth because the craft travels on the cushion of air beneath it.

The first model of a hovercraft was built in the mid 1950s by a British inventor named Christopher Cockerill. The first full-sized hovercraft was tested in 1959. Today, many hovercraft operate as ferries to carry people and cars across the water. The largest hovercraft in operation weighs over 305 tons and can carry up to 418 passengers and 60 vehicles. It has four gas-turbine engines and can travel up to 75 mph (120 km/h). It is the fastest large sea-going craft in the world.

Hovercraft are unique because they can travel over both land and water. They are especially useful in waterways that are too shallow for regular boats to travel in. And they are ideal as ferries because they can come right up onto the land to load and unload passengers and vehicles.

Hovercraft operations are treated like and operate more like an airline than a shipping line. Passenger seats are very similar to those used on passenger airlines. Also, instead of having a wheelhouse or a pilot house, a hovercraft has a cabin called the flight deck. This is where the pilot sits to drive the hovercraft.

A hovercraft can float because downward moving air creates an upward force. Many aircraft also use this principle. Helicopters have rotating blades with airfoil shapes that push air downward. This creates an upward force on the blades. When this force is greater than the weight of the helicopter it will lift into the air. When the force is equal to the weight of the craft it will hover in the air similarly to a hovercraft.

Helicopter

The osprey (middle photo) is an aircraft that combines the speed of an airplane with the maneuverability of a helicopter. The rotors of the osprey can be tilted. When they are in the vertical position they act like helicopter blades, pushing air down to create lift. Once the aircraft has taken off, the rotors can be tilted forward to act as propellers to create thrust while the airflow over the wings provides the needed lift. The rotors are so long that they must be tilted up for landing, so the craft lands vertically like a helicopter. Ospreys are used primarily as troop transports for the military and may replace helicopters in many applications.

Osprey

Another military vehicle that has the ability to hover and to do vertical take-offs and landings is the harrier jet (lower photo). The harrier has one large jet engine, but it has what is called a vectored thrust system. This system can direct the gases that come out of the jet engine in any direction. If the gases are directed downward, the plane can move verti-

Harrier

MAKING A FLOATER

Purpose: To make a simple model of an air-cushioned vehicle

Materials: hole punch, paper or Styrofoam plate, soda straw

Procedure:

1. Punch a hole in the center of a paper or Styrofoam plate just large enough for a soda straw.

2. Stick a soda straw through the bottom of the plate.

3. Place the plate on a flat surface and blow gently in the straw and watch the plate float across the surface.

cally or even hover. If the gases are directed toward the back of the plane, it can fly forward very fast. If the gases are directed toward the front of the plane, it can even fly backwards.

All of these vehicles are faster and more efficient than traditional wheeled or water vehicles because they use the power of air to lift the vehicle above the surface to reduce friction. ■

WHAT DID WE LEARN?

- What is an ACV?
- How are hovercraft different from other vehicles?
- Why are hovercraft preferable to traditional boats in certain areas?
- Why are hovercraft more energy efficient than many other vehicles?

TAKING IT FURTHER

- Which of Newton's laws of motion are most easily seen in the operation of hovercraft?
- How are harrier jets similar to hovercraft?

REDUCING FRICTION

Another vehicle that floats above the water is a hydrofoil. However, a **hydrofoil** does not float on the air like a hovercraft. Instead, it uses Bernoulli's principle to create lift in the water just as airplanes do to create lift in the air.

When a hydrofoil is not moving it appears to be a normal boat. But attached to the boat under the water are airfoil-shaped wings. As the craft begins to move through the water, the water passing over the top of the underwater wings moves more quickly than the water

under the wings, thus creating lift. As the craft goes faster, this force is actually enough to lift the hull out of the water and the whole craft moves on the wings as it is driven forward by an engine in the water. By lifting the hull out of the water, the friction between the hull and the water is greatly reduced, so less force is needed for the craft to move through the water.

Reducing friction is important regardless of whether the craft moves through the water, on top of the water, or flies through the air.

Engineers and scientists work very hard to make vehicles that have as little friction as possible. The shape and smoothness of the surface of the vehicle contribute greatly to the amount of friction it experiences.

Purpose: To visualize how water and air flow around different shapes to find the most efficient shape

Materials: modeling clay, toothpick, cardboard, pitcher

Procedure:

1. Form modeling clay into different geometric shapes. Each shape should be approximately two inches long and ½-inch thick. Make a circle, a square, a star, and a teardrop. You can make other shapes as well if you like.

2. Stick a toothpick through the center of each shape and attach the shapes to a piece of cardboard in a row near the top edge.

3. Place the cardboard with the shapes over a sink and tip the cardboard up at a nearly vertical angle.

4. Using a pitcher, slowly pour water down the cardboard so that it flows onto one of the shapes. Repeat this for each shape.

5. Watch the path that the water takes around each shape. Be sure to try turning the shapes in different orientations to see which direction is most efficient.

Questions:

- Which shapes appear to allow the water to flow most easily?

- Which shapes seem to hinder the flow of the water?

- How can you apply what you learned from this experiment to the desired shape for a vehicle?

UNIT 3

MILITARY INVENTIONS

HISTORICAL MILITARY WEAPONS

The physics of war

What kinds of weapons have people invented?

Words to know:

ballista

Challenge words:

first-class lever

second-class lever

third-class lever

Inventions and technology are certainly not limited to the Industrial Revolution. God created people to be creative like Him, and men and women have been using that creativity to invent the things they need ever since Adam and Eve left the Garden. It has been said that necessity is the mother of invention. If someone feels there is a need for a machine to do something, they, or someone else, will probably find a way to invent a machine to do it.

Since the earliest times, man has had the knowledge to do metal working. Genesis 4:22 says that Tubal-Cain was a man who forged tools from bronze and iron. Tubal-Cain was just a few generations after Adam. So we see that inventions have been around since the beginning of man. People have invented items for every conceivable purpose from music to farming, from cooking to transportation. Sadly, some of the most incredible inventions have been devised specifically for use in war. On the positive side, people have taken what they have learned from making military weapons and used that knowledge for peaceful purposes as well. For example, the rocket was originally invented for military uses, but has since been used for a multitude of other applications. Similarly, what was learned from the building of the great war machines of Greece and Rome led to many peaceful applications as well.

Some of the earliest weapons were those formed from metal such as spears and shields. Also, bows and arrows played an important role in early warfare. These kinds of weapons were used in nearly every ancient civilization from Egypt to Japan, and from Babylon to India. Also, many of these cultures developed chariots and other vehicles for moving troops and equipment. What people learned from making these early weapons was later applied to more advanced weapons.

The Greeks and Romans used this knowledge, as well as their understanding of physical principles, to develop siege weapons. One of the greatest inventors of the ancient world was Archimedes, who lived in the third century BC. Archimedes was a mathematician who applied what he learned to help defend the city of Syracuse. He developed catapults that used the lever principle to launch huge stones at approaching troops. He also developed large levers that could actually tip over an enemy ship in the harbor. He used a system of ropes and pulleys to lift enemy ships out of the water as well. When the Romans captured Syracuse, they took many of Archimedes' ideas and learned to build similar weapons themselves.

The Roman army used catapults and ballistae as their main siege weapons. Many of the catapults used a winding mechanism to pull back on the lever arm. When the force was removed, the arm threw the rock or other weight toward the enemy. Romans also used a ballista, a weapon that was like a giant cross-bow that could launch a large javelin over a great distance.

Many of these weapons were improved and used during the Middle Ages. However, one invention made most of the older weapons obsolete. That invention was gunpowder. Once gunpowder was introduced, weapons that could only be used at close range were no longer effective. Gunpowder is such an important invention that we will study it more in the next lesson.

Since the advent of gunpowder, military inventions have become more high tech. Fire-

A Roman catapult

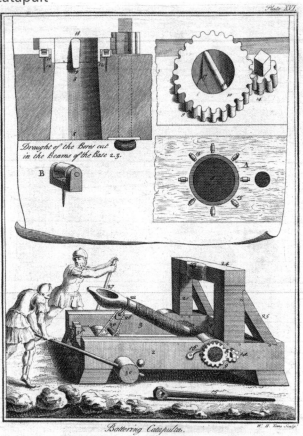

TESTING CATAPULTS

Purpose: To make a simple catapult

Materials: ruler, small block, eraser

Procedure:

1. In an open area, place a ruler on top of a small block.

2. Place a small eraser on one end of the ruler.

3. Push down quickly on the other end of the ruler. This will make the eraser go flying.

Experiment with different locations of the block with respect to the eraser. Also, use different amounts of force when you push down on the ruler. Which combination causes the eraser to fly the farthest? Set up a target and see if you can hit it with the eraser.

arms have become more precise and more deadly. From early flintlock guns to modern day assault rifles, gunpowder changed the face of war. Artillery such as cannons replaced catapults and ballistae. And with the invention of rockets, explosives can now be sent from any location in the world to anywhere else in the world.

As we mentioned at the beginning of the lesson, the knowledge gained from the development of military weapons has helped in the development of many other peace-time applications as well. The art of fireworks is possible because of the development of gunpowder. Also, guns made survival in the wilderness much easier. And civilian applications are abundant for sonar, radar, and submarine technology, as we will see in later lessons. ■

WHAT DID WE LEARN?

- What were some of the earliest weapons invented?

- What military invention was the most revolutionary?

- What kinds of weapons were used by the Romans?

TAKING IT FURTHER

- What are some ways that military technology has helped people?

- Name at least two inventions not listed in the lesson that have both military and civilian applications.

LEVERS

Catapults operate on the lever principle. There are three basic kinds of levers. A **first-class lever** has the weight at one end, the fulcrum in the middle, and the effort applied at the other end. This is the kind of lever you made in the activity above. A **second-class lever** has the weight in the middle and the fulcrum and effort at opposite ends, like a wheelbarrow. A **third-class lever** has the weight at one end and the fulcrum at the other, with the effort applied in the middle.

Design a catapult that uses a third-class lever and tell why it is a better design for a catapult than a first-class lever. For more detailed information on levers, see the lessons in *God's Design for the Physical World: Machines and Motion*.

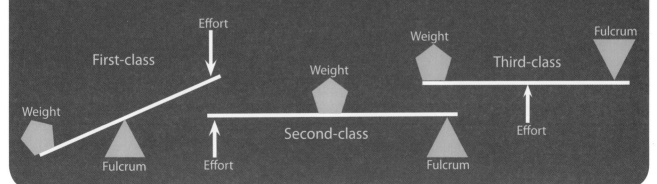

GUNPOWDER

It's explosive

LESSON 18

Why is gunpowder explosive?

Words to know:

ballistics

Challenge words:

smooth bore

rifled

One of the most important military inventions was gunpowder. The origin of gunpowder is not completely clear. We know that gunpowder was discovered by the Chinese. Some sources believe it may have been used as early as AD 300; however, records indicate that it was not common, even in China, until about 850.

Gunpowder is a combination of three important ingredients: sulfur, saltpeter (potassium nitrate), and carbon, usually in the form of charcoal. When these three ingredients are mixed together they burn explosively. No one knows exactly how this phenomenon was discovered, but we know that the Chinese used this substance initially for fireworks. It wasn't until the twelfth century that the Chinese began using gunpowder to fire rockets and to send bombs against their enemies.

The Chinese initially used bamboo cannons to fire rocks and metal balls. They also made the first metal-barreled gun. But a weapon like this is not easy to keep secret. The recipe for gunpowder traveled with merchants along the Silk Road from China to Europe. The English scientist Sir Roger Bacon recorded having the recipe for making gunpowder in 1267. From that time on, it was just a matter of testing, experimenting, and improving to make weapons using this new discovery.

Originally, cannons were developed to replace catapults. The first metal cannons were used around 1350. Large artillery was the obvious first use of gunpowder from a military perspective. However, cannons are heavy and difficult to move, so smaller pieces were developed. Eventually personal weapons were created. The earliest guns were matchlock guns that used a slow-burning fuse to ignite the gunpowder. There were several problems with a matchlock gun. First, you had to light it ahead of time; second, it glowed at night so the enemy could see you; and third, the fuse could go out just when you needed it most. Also, a spark could set off a charge too soon and was dangerous for the person shooting the gun, so better methods were developed. In about 1650, the flintlock firing mechanism, like the one shown here, was designed. The flintlock gun used a spark from a piece of flint to ignite the gunpowder. The spark was generated when the operator pulled the trigger. The flintlock gun was the main military weapon from the middle of the seventeenth century into the nineteenth century.

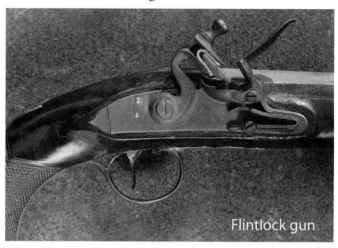
Flintlock gun

One of the first problems with gunpowder was finding a way to keep all three ingredients mixed equally. The lighter carbon worked its way to the top of the mixture and the heavier saltpeter settled to the bottom. It was discovered that the three ingredients could be mixed together with a liquid and then dried into pellets called grains. This greatly improved the performance of the gunpowder.

Once guns and gunpowder became readily available and somewhat reliable, most of the older military weapons became obsolete. Cannons replaced catapults and ballista, rifles replaced swords and spears. A whole new area of science was necessary to efficiently use these new weapons. This field of physics is called **ballistics**. Ballistics experts study the paths of moving objects. Cannonballs and bullets do not make a straight path through the air. Because of the pull of gravity, a cannonball will move in

IMPROVING GUNPOWDER

Purpose: To understand how gunpowder was improved

Materials: popcorn kernels, uncooked rice, flour

Procedure:

1. Place 2 tablespoons of popcorn kernels, 2 tablespoons of uncooked rice, and 2 tablespoons of flour in a bowl.

2. Stir the mixture together. These three ingredients represent the three ingredients that are used to make gunpowder. When the gunpowder was thoroughly mixed it usually worked pretty well, but it didn't stay mixed.

3. Slowly shake the bowl back and forth. What do you see happening? The popcorn kernels are not as dense as the other ingredients so they rise to the top. The flour is denser than the other ingredients so it settles to the bottom.

4. Now, mix a small amount of water into the mixture to form a paste. Be sure to mix all the ingredients well.

5. Spread the mixture on a piece of foil and allow the mixture to dry. Now you can break the dried paste into smaller pieces that contain all three ingredients, and all three ingredients will stay together.

Conclusion: This is how gunpowder was improved. Obviously, your grains are much larger than grains of gun powder, but the idea is the same. If you have some extra popcorn, you can cook it and hear the sounds of gunpowder, then enjoy a fun snack.

an arc. Its forward motion is due to the force of the gunpowder, while its downward motion is due to the force of gravity. Therefore, artillery experts must learn to compensate for the force of gravity in order to hit the desired target. ■

Military Inventions

WHAT DID WE LEARN?

- Who first discovered gunpowder?
- How was gunpowder first used?
- What is ballistics?
- What were some problems with the matchlock gun?

TAKING IT FURTHER

- How was gunpowder made more reliable?
- How is a cannon similar to a catapult?
- How is a cannon different from a catapult?
- How might gunpowder be used for peaceful purposes?

IMPROVING ACCURACY

Making a gun is a very complicated process. The flintlock guns were forged by blacksmiths to exacting standards for their day. The flintlock gun used in the American Revolution was called the Brown Bess. Most of these guns had a **smooth-bore** barrel. This means that the inside of the barrel was completely smooth. A smooth-bore barrel is made by drilling down the center of the barrel with bigger and bigger bits until the hole is the desired size.

Then the inside is polished to ensure that it is smooth. Shotguns have smooth-bored barrels.

Most guns today, however, have rifled barrels. A **rifled** barrel has a spiraling groove cut into the inside of the barrel. When the gun is fired, the bullet moves along this groove inside the barrel and begins to spin very quickly, making the bullet more accurate. Why does a rifled barrel improve performance? In which sport does the player spin the ball to improve accuracy?

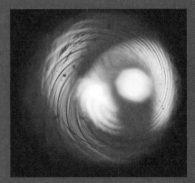

This is an image of a .35 Remington, microgroove rifled barrel with a right hand twist.

TANK

A modern day chariot

How does a tank move?

Much of the technology we see in modern automobiles grew out of the work done to develop military tanks in World War II. But where did the idea of tanks come from? The earliest military vehicles were chariots. Chariots were developed in the Mesopotamia area about 2000 BC. They were used extensively in the Middle East by 1700 BC and had spread to Asia and Europe by about 1500 BC. King Cyrus of Persia is recorded to have used chariots in battle in the 6th century BC. King Cyrus used smaller chariots that could carry four archers to blast through the enemy's lines. He also used larger chariots pulled by oxen that could carry twenty soldiers. These vehicles allowed the soldiers improved mobility while giving them the opportunity to shoot arrows and throw javelins at a stunned enemy.

Relief of Ramses II at the Battle of Kadesh, 13th century BC

Another early "vehicle" that gave the army striking power, mobility, and armor was the war elephant. Elephants were primarily used in Southeast Asia and Africa where they were readily available. But after fighting in India in 327 BC, Alexander the Great decided to incorporate war elephants into his army as well.

The chariot and the war elephant both attempted to meet the need for armored troops that could move quickly and strike into the heart of the enemy lines, but better mobility was needed. This led to the development of armored soldiers on armored horses. These soldiers had many of the advantages of the chariot and war elephant without many of the disadvantages, such as wheels

that got stuck or elephants that turned and trampled their own troops. Thus, the armored cavalry became one of the most important parts of any army for over 1,000 years.

This changed, however, in the 14th century with the invention of firearms. As guns and cannons became more powerful, traditional armor no longer provided adequate protection and eventually became obsolete. The mobility of the horse was still important, but soldiers were vulnerable to enemy fire. For the next 500 years, man concentrated on making better firearms but did little to improve protection for the soldiers.

Then, in the middle of the Civil War, a discovery was made that may seem to have little to do with tanks, but actually sparked an important idea. A very famous battle occurred on March 8–9, 1862, between two ships, the *Monitor* and the *Merrimack*. What made this battle so famous was that it was the first battle between iron-clad ships. Before that time, ships were primarily made from wood. Now what does this have to do with tanks, you may ask? Well, once iron-clad ships became more common, people began to wonder if an iron-clad vehicle could be made for land that could transport troops safely on land. Thus the idea of a tank was born.

THE ADVANTAGE OF TRACKS

Purpose: To see why tracks are necessary for tanks

Materials: modeling clay, two spools of thread, craft sticks, books

Procedure:

1. Roll out some modeling clay into a 4-inch square pad.

2. Place 2 spools of thread on their sides on the clay as shown below (only without the sticks) to represent the wheels of a vehicle. Do not press the spools into the clay.

3. Lay a heavy book across the spools of thread.

4. Now lift the book off and remove the spools. Observe the indentations in the clay.

5. Next, smooth out the clay and place two craft sticks on the clay and set the spools sideways on top of the sticks as shown.

6. Place the book on top of the spools as before.

7. Lift off the book and the spools. Pick up the craft sticks and observe the indentations in the clay.

Questions: How are the indentations different? Why are they shallower when the sticks are used? How is this similar to the treads on a tank?

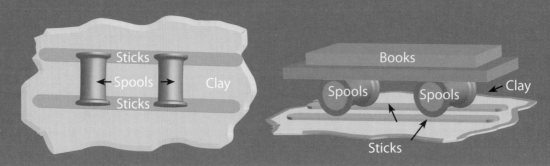

There was one major problem with making iron-clad land vehicles. The weight would cause the wheels to become stuck or to break down. Thus, it was another fifty years before the tank was actually built. In the years leading up to World War I, a British soldier named Ernest Swinton saw many battles in which the machine gun was used to mow down hundreds of soldiers. He was determined to find a way to protect soldiers. In 1914 he heard from a friend in South Africa about a farm machine that did not move on wheels. This machine used caterpillar tracks to spread out the weight of the tractor and thus keep the vehicle from getting stuck in uneven terrain. Swinton knew this could be the design that was needed to build an armored land vehicle.

With the help of Winston Churchill, Swinton convinced the British military to design and build a tracked armored vehicle. The first working tank was built in 1915, and was called "Little Willie." It had room for eight crew members and a large gun turret on top. Unfortunately, the track design had problems and the turret made the tank top heavy. So the vehicle was redesigned and became "Big Willie." This larger tank had six cannons, or four cannons and two machine guns. The first of these machines was used in battle on September 15, 1916. Although there were many problems to be worked out, every nation involved in the war quickly realized the advantages of armored vehicles that could cross barbed wire and trenches and open a path for foot soldiers.

Since World War I, tanks have grown in size and speed. They have also grown in firepower. The premier battle tank today is the American M1 Abrams tank (M1A1). This tank can fire a 120 mm shell that can penetrate an enemy tank. It uses laser-guidance technology and thermal-imaging sights to guarantee that the shell nearly always hits the target. The Abrams uses a gas-turbine engine, similar to a helicopter engine, to drive the tracks of the tank. Other smaller tanks are also important to modern warfare. M2 and M3 Bradley fighting vehicles can not only travel over most land, but they can also "swim" with the aid of canvas water barriers. So today, the military does not rely on horses, but on tanks to provide striking power and mobility for its soldiers. ■

M1A1 Abrams Tank

M3A1 Bradley Fighting Vehicle

WHAT DID WE LEARN?

- What is the purpose of a tank in warfare?

- What are two of the earliest war vehicles?

- What invention made traditional armor useless?

- What invention made tanks possible?

- When were the first military tanks invented?

TAKING IT FURTHER

- Why is the track system necessary for a tank?

- How can airplanes take the place of tanks in some battles?

- Why are tanks still necessary?

GASOLINE VS. DIESEL

The M1 Abrams tank currently uses a gasoline turbine engine. This engine provides power to allow the tank to travel over nearly any terrain at speeds never dreamed of in World War I. Speed and power are the main advantages of the gasoline engine. However, some people think that a diesel engine would be a better choice for the tank.

In any design project, the engineer must make some decisions that do not have clear answers. She must weigh the advantages and disadvantages of each decision. If a diesel engine were chosen, there would be some advantages. The diesel engine is more efficient so less fuel is needed to go the same distance. The diesel engine is less expensive. Also, the diesel engine

puts out less heat so it is harder for heat seeking missiles to find the target. But diesel engines have more trouble performing well in cold weather. They are bigger and heavier than gasoline engines and do not provide as much power, so they are slower.

If you were the engineer in charge, which engine would you choose and why?

SUBMARINE

Underwater boat

LESSON
20

How does a submarine stay underwater?

Words to know:

submarine

buoyancy

ballast

screw

rudder

dive plane

hull

Challenge words:

submersible

What is a submarine? A submarine is an underwater craft. Submarines were originally designed to be military warships. But today, submarines are not only used for military purposes, but also for exploration of the ocean.

How submarines work

The idea of a submarine has been around for hundreds of years, but there were many problems to be solved before a working submarine could be built. The first problem to be solved was buoyancy. Buoyancy is the force exerted by liquids and gases equal to the mass of the displaced fluid. The buoyancy of an object is related to its density. If something is less dense than water, it will float on the surface. If it is denser than the water, it will sink. Before a submarine could be built, a way had to be found to change the density of the ship in order to make it sink and rise as necessary. Other problems included getting fresh air into the ship, making the ship water tight under pressure, and propelling the ship through the water. All of these problems were solved over time.

The most difficult problem to solve was the buoyancy problem. An Englishman named William Bourne suggested the idea of ballasting in 1578. Ballast is a material that you carry in your craft that you can get rid of when necessary to change the weight and thus the density of your vehicle. Early hot air balloon pilots used this idea. They would carry bags of sand or other materials and throw sand out of the basket to make the balloon lighter when they wanted the balloon to rise. Submarines use this idea to make the sub rise and sink as well. But instead of using sand, the submarine uses air and seawater.

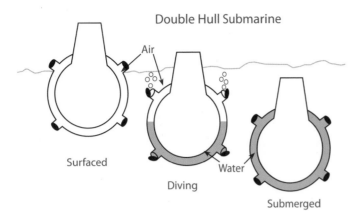

Double Hull Submarine

Surfaced

Air

Diving

Water

Submerged

A submarine has special tanks called ballast tanks that are filled with air when the sub is on the surface of the water. When the submarine is ready to dive, seawater is pumped into the tanks, forcing the air out. Since the water is heavier than the air, the submarine becomes heavier and begins to sink. When the sub needs to rise, compressed air is released into the ballast tanks, forcing water out. This causes the submarine to become lighter, so it rises. Although the idea of ballasting had been around since 1578, the process was not really perfected until the 19th century.

Military use of submarines

The first military use of a submarine was during the American Revolutionary War. In 1776 a small vehicle called the *Turtle* was designed by a man named David Bushnell to carry one man under water. The *Turtle* had hand cranks to propel it through the water. The operator used the *Turtle* to maneuver next to a British warship, where he tried to attach a bomb. He was unsuccessful in planting the bomb, but his trip underwater made history as the first military use of a submarine. The first successful military battle using a submarine occurred in 1864, when a Confederate sub called the *Hunley* sank a Union warship.

Power systems

Early submarines were driven by human power. Many had hand or foot cranks that turned propellers, which in turn pushed the vehicle through the water. Then in 1898 John Philip Holland developed the first successful gasoline/electric driven submarine. Today, many submarines use diesel/electric engines

> ## FUN FACT
>
> Robert Fulton, the developer of the steam-driven paddle wheel boat, worked with Napoleon Bonaparte to design a submarine that was powered by a surface sail. However, Napoleon became distracted with other ideas and did not follow up on Fulton's design.

The Turtle

The Hunley

FUN FACT

German U-boats, underwater boats, were one of the most feared elements of World War I. A German U-boat shocked the world when it sunk the luxury liner RMS *Lusitania* on May 7, 1915.

The Seawolf-class nuclear-powered attack submarine *Jimmy Carter* (SSN 23) underway during sea trials

for power. The diesel engines are used when the submarine is on the surface. These engines also charge electric batteries. When the submarine submerges, it uses the batteries for power. Electric batteries are much quieter than the diesel engine, making it more difficult to detect the submarine when it is underwater.

More recent submarines use nuclear reactors to provide the necessary power. Nuclear subs have many advantages over diesel subs. First, because the reactors are heavier than the diesel engines, the subs must be larger to create buoyancy. This may not seem like an advantage, but for the men and women who must live and work on the sub, it is nice to have more room. Also, nuclear subs can stay submerged indefinitely. The only limit being how much food can be carried for the crew. There are no diesel fumes for the crew to breathe and the electricity provided by the nuclear reactors also powers air purifiers to keep the air from becoming stale. Nuclear submarines are very expensive, but play a vital role in America's naval arsenal.

TESTING BUOYANCY

Purpose: To see how buoyancy is related to pressure

Materials: 2-liter bottle, ketchup packets

Procedure:

1. Fill a 2-liter bottle most of the way with water.

2. Push 3 or 4 ketchup packets, the kind you get at a fast food restaurant, into the bottle.

Make sure the packets have a little extra air in them, they should not be flat. The packets should float because they have a little air inside which makes them buoyant.

3. Next, screw the cap on tightly and squeeze the sides of the bottle. What happened?

Conclusion: Squeezing the bottle increases the pressure inside the

bottle. The increased pressure should make the packets non-buoyant by compressing the air, and they should begin to sink.

Buoyancy is a result of relative densities. When something is less dense than the water, it floats; when it is denser, it sinks. This is why submarines can sink when their ballast tanks are filled with water, and rise when they are filled with air.

God designed the first true ballasting system. A sea creature called the nautilus has a double shell. It lives in the outer shell and uses the inner shell as a ballast tank. It allows water into the shell when it wants to sink and pumps the water out with gases stored in the inner shell when it wants to rise. Because the nautilus uses a similar design to submarines, a very popular name for a submarine is the *Nautilus*.

Parts of a submarine

A submarine has many important parts in addition to the ballast tanks and the engines. The engines must drive one or more propellers. On a submarine the propellers are called screws. Some subs have several screws, but most have one large propeller. The submarine also has a rudder at the back of the ship to help with steering; and it has dive planes, which are like wings that help to stabilize the ship and direct the ship up and down in the water. The hull is also a very important part of the ship. The hull is the outside of the ship. Most submarines have a double hull so that if there is a problem with the outer hull, the ship can still surface safely. Finally, the communications systems are vital to submarines. Radio and sonar are both used for communication and help the people on the submarine to perform their duties. ■

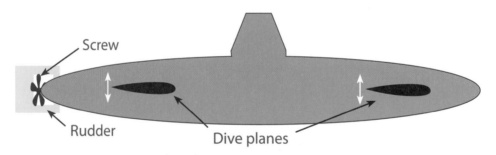

Screw

Rudder

Dive planes

WHAT DID WE LEARN?

- What is a submarine?
- What were some of the problems that had to be solved in order to make a successful submarine?
- What is ballast?
- What material is used as ballast on a submarine?
- What kind of vehicle used ballast before submarines?
- When was the first submarine used in a battle?

TAKING IT FURTHER

- How were the first submarines powered?
- List three advantages of nuclear submarines.
- Why does a nuclear submarine have more living space than a diesel submarine?
- How does ballasting work on a submarine?
- Why are submarines useful in warfare?
- Why are electric batteries used under water rather than diesel engines?

SUBMERSIBLES

Although submarines were invented for military uses, the technology has been used to build many submarines and **submersibles** that are used for ocean exploration. Submarines are designed to operate up to 2,000 feet (610 m) below the surface of the ocean. Below this level, the pressure caused by the weight of the water above becomes too great for most submarines. The deeper you go, the greater the water pressure. For military purposes, there is really no advantage to going much deeper than 2,000 feet (610 m). But from a scientific perspective, there is much to learn at greater depths. Therefore, submersibles have been developed that can go much deeper than an ordinary submarine.

Most submersibles are non-manned vehicles that can withstand great pressure. They usually have cameras and

Alvin

other equipment that can send information back to the research vessel on the surface. Submersibles also often have robotic arms that can collect samples from the water or bottom of the ocean. The vehicle, as well as the cameras and robotic arms, are all remotely controlled by the operators on the surface.

One of the most famous submersibles used today is called

Alvin. Alvin was developed in 1964, but is still being used by scientists to study the world's oceans. Alvin can dive as deep as 14,000 feet (4,267 m) and has been used to explore the *Titanic* and other shipwrecks as well as many different parts of the ocean floor. Alvin was the submersible being used when giant tube worms were discovered on the floor of the ocean near heat vents.

Purpose: To appreciate how deep submersibles can go

Materials: piece of paper, pencil

Procedure:

1. Draw a vertical line 10½ inches long in the center of a piece of paper.

2. Mark the top of the line as the surface of the ocean.

3. Make marks every ½ inch going down the line. Each mark represents 1,000 feet.

4. Label each mark showing the depth. You should have 21 marks for 21,000 feet on your line.

5. Place the following information on your chart by drawing a small picture and labeling each item at the appropriate depth.

The first submarine, built by Holland in 1898, could only go 108 feet below the surface. A scuba diver can dive down to 475 feet. A nuclear sub usually operates at about 985 feet. The URN Deep Submergence Rescue Vehicle can dive down to 2,460 feet. The deepest submarine can operate at 2,953 feet. Alvin can dive down 14,000 feet. The *Nautilus* submersible can dive to 19,685 feet, and the Japanese submersible *Shinkai* can dive to 21,325 feet.

Radar & Sonar

Reflectors

LESSON

21

How does radar and sonar work?

Words to know:

radar

sonar

passive sonar

active sonar

acoustic communication sonar

Challenge words:

Doppler radar

Doppler effect

One of the most important military inventions of the twentieth century is radar. This invention is important not only because it changed the face of warfare, but because of all the non-military applications that grew out of the radar research. Today, radar plays a very important role in commercial airlines, geological surveying, meteorology, and astronomy, as well as in military applications.

The word radar is an acronym for RAdio Detection And Ranging. Radar was first developed between 1935 and 1940 by several countries simultaneously. One of the earliest radar systems was built in 1935 by Sir Robert Alexander Watson-Watt of Scotland. A radar system has two main parts. The first part is a transmitter. The transmitter sends out a radio signal. Most radar systems transmit in the microwave frequency range, but some systems use other frequencies as well. The second part of the system is the receiver. The receiver detects radio waves in the same frequency range that the transmitter generates.

The radio waves that are sent out will continue traveling in a straight line from the transmitter until they encounter an object. If the object is solid, some of the energy will be reflected back toward the transmitter. The receiver will detect this reflected energy. Most radar systems take the detected energy and translate it into a visual picture such as a line or a dot indicating where the object is.

The time between when the signal is sent and when the reflection is received is the time it takes for the signal to travel to the detected object and back. We know that distance is equal to the rate or speed at which the signal travels multiplied by the time is takes to get there. So, using the speed at which the radio waves travel, it is possible to determine how far away something is from the time

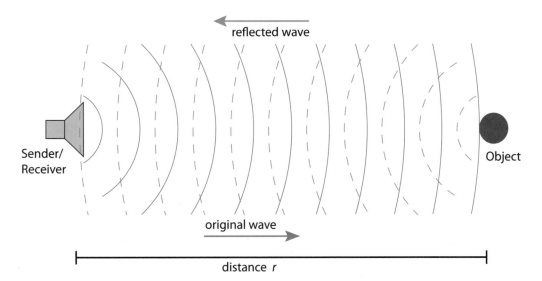

original wave

distance *r*

it takes for the signal to bounce back. Radar systems have computers that automatically calculate these distances.

Since World War II, radar systems have been, and continue to be, used by the military to detect enemy ships, airplanes, and other objects such as missiles. Radar is an indispensable part of nearly every military vehicle and outpost.

Radar was so successful in the air and on land that is was only natural to adapt it for use underwater to detect submarines. Sonar was developed specifically for use underwater. Sonar stands for SOund Navigation And Ranging, and operates on the same basic principles as radar. However, instead of transmitting a microwave radio signal a sonar system transmits an ultrasonic sound wave. The sound waves travel through the water and reflect off of solid objects. These reflected sound waves are detected by the sonar system and translated into pictures.

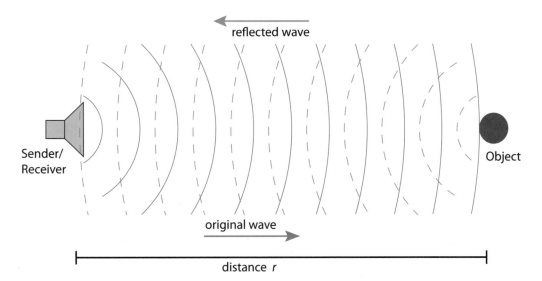

FUN FACT

Whales and dolphins use sonar to communicate with other whales and dolphins. Therefore, it is important for sonar operators to be able to distinguish between animal sounds and submarine sounds.

Submarines often have three different types of sonar systems. Passive sonar only uses the detecting part of the system. It detects sound waves and is used primarily to listen for other subs. A passive sonar array is a series of detectors that are towed behind the submarine. Because it does not generate the sound waves it detects, the distance to the detected object can only be estimated, but it can still be an effective tool.

Submarines also have active sonar systems that can send out a ping, which is a loud sound that travels at approximately 5,000 feet per second (1,500 meters per second). The ping will reflect off of surrounding objects and show the sonar operator what is in the area. The sound can be sent in various directions and at various frequencies to help distinguish between natural wildlife and enemy subs.

A third type of sonar often found on submarines is acoustic communication sonar. This is a system that allows submarines to talk to each other. Sound signals much like Morse code are sent from one sub to another where the receiver on the second ship translates the sounds into words.

USING RADAR

Complete the "Sonar" worksheet to gain a small understanding of how radar and sonar can be used.

Today, radar and sonar have a whole host of applications. Of course, there are many military applications. Radar is used to detect aircraft. It is also used to detect and track missiles. But radar is also used in the commercial airline industry. It is used to detect obstacles in the aircraft's path, and radar also gives accurate altitude measurements. One of the most important uses of radar is fog radar. Because radar does not depend on visibility, it can be used to guide aircraft during take-off and landing when there is fog. Fog radar was first developed in 1960, and is a vital resource at airports that often have foggy weather.

A sonar image of an ocean floor ridge

Radar and sonar are also important for navigation and mapping purposes. Radar is used to map the surface of the earth and sonar is used to map the floor of the oceans. Much of what we have learned about what is below the surface of the water has been learned by sonar mapping. Sonar is also used to search for sunken vessels and other items on the ocean floor. Sonar is even used by fishermen to detect schools of fish.

Meteorologists use radar extensively to map storms. Radar can be used to generate a visual image to see what is going on inside a storm and to predict the development of tornadoes. Also, radar is used to track the movements of hurricanes. Radar can measure the development of precipitation and is vital for modern weather forecasting.

Finally, one of the most exciting uses of radar is in the field of astronomy. Radar signals can be used to accurately measure distances to objects in space. The distance to the moon was first measured with radar in 1946. The distance to Venus was measured in 1958, and the distance to the sun was measured in 1959. Radar is also used to track solar flares. Radar signals are used for communication with astronauts and equipment in outer space. And radar telescopes are used to detect the activity of distant stars. Radar and sonar are very important to many areas of our lives. ■

FUN FACT

Bats use sonar by sending out a high-pitched sound, then listening for the echoes reflected from nearby surfaces and objects. By detecting its own reflected sounds, often among other distracting noises, the small mammal is able to avoid obstacles and obtain the information necessary for tracking and catching an insect.

WHAT DID WE LEARN?

- What is radar?
- What is sonar?
- When was radar first developed?
- What are the two main parts of a radar system?

TAKING IT FURTHER

- Why do military submarines have a passive radar system?
- Why must a radar system divide by two the time from the transmission of the signal until the echo is received in order to determine the distance to the object?
- How can a sonar system be used to detect objects without being confused by the floor of the ocean?
- Why might it be important for a commercial airline to use radar to detect its exact altitude?

DOPPLER RADAR

Meteorologists use a special type of radar called **Doppler radar** to track storms. Doppler radar derives its name from the **Doppler effect**.

The Doppler effect was first described in 1842 by an Austrian physicist named Johann Christian Doppler who noticed that light from distant objects in space was color-shifted—the light was a different color than was expected. After much work, he was able to mathematically describe how this shift occurs. Later, he realized that this same effect occurs with sound.

You may have noticed that the pitch of a siren or train horn changes as it approaches and then goes away from you. This is because of the Doppler effect. Essentially, because of the Doppler effect, the frequency of sound or light waves that are generated by an object that is approaching you will be higher because the waves are being compressed. Similarly, the frequency of light or sound waves generated by an object that is moving away from you will be lower because the waves are being stretched out as the object moves away.

Because the frequency of a reflected radio wave is higher than the original generated wave if it reflects off of an object that is moving toward the radar system, and lower if the object is moving away from the radar system, Doppler radar systems can calculate the speed at which an object is moving. This is very important in studying weather systems. If one part of the storm is moving away from the radar system and another part of the storm is moving toward the radar system, this could indicate that a spiraling motion is taking place inside the cloud. If the storm is beginning to spiral, it could mean

A Doppler radar at the National Storm Prediction Center in Norman, Oklahoma

that conditions are right for a tornado to develop. Also, Doppler radar helps meteorologists measure how fast a storm is moving and in what direction it is moving. This allows the National Weather Service to issue more accurate warnings and could ultimately save lives.

Question: What other applications can you think of for Doppler radar?

ELECTRIC LIGHT

A bright idea

How was the light bulb invented?

Words to know:

incandescence

arc lights

inert gases

Challenge words:

halogen bulb

fluorescent bulb

light-emitting diode/LED

Have you ever had the electricity go out in your home at night? You may have been instantly plunged into darkness. What did you do? Did you find a flashlight to turn on or light some candles? Many of us cannot imagine life without electricity and especially without the electric light. But the electric light has only been a reality in homes for a little more than 100 years. Prior to the invention of the electric light, people lit their homes with candles, or gas or oil lamps.

But all this changed in 1879, when Thomas Edison and his group of "muckers" developed the first incandescent light bulb. Before Edison was even born, work had been done on the electric light. Sir Humphry Davy, an English scientist, discovered that an electric current passed through certain metals would cause those metals to glow. This is the idea of incandescence. Later, Michael Faraday, a student of Davy's, experimented with electricity and magnetism and developed the idea of electromagnetic rotation, which is the basis of the electric motor and the electric generator. These experiments, along with many others, set the stage for the development of the incandescent light.

In the early 1870s some cities had begun using an electric lighting system called arc lighting. Arc lights produced a glow when an arc of electricity jumped between two carbon rods. Arc lights were used for street lights in some areas. However, arc lights were not suitable for home use. They gave off a harsh light that was too intense for indoor use, and they were very smelly. So a better system was needed.

By 1878 Thomas Edison was already a well-known inventor, having created a stock ticker, an electric vote recorder, the phonograph, and many other inventions. But he set to work to develop what would become his most famous invention. He wanted to develop a useful indoor electric lighting system. And the first part of that invention was a reliable incandescent bulb.

Edison knew that he and the people who worked for him, whom he affectionately referred to as muckers, had to solve two major problems. First, they had to develop a glass bulb that could have all the air pumped out so that the filament did not burn up with the oxygen in the air. And second, they had to find a filament that would glow for many hours when electricity was flowing through it. Some of the workers worked on a method to remove the air. They eventually developed a special vacuum pump that could remove the air from a sealed glass bulb.

Other workers tested different materials for the filament. All together, Edison's lab tested over 1,600 different materials before they found the best one. Some of the materials they tried included horse hair, coconut fibers, fishing line, and even spider web. But in the fall of 1879, Edison determined that a piece of cotton sewing thread that was first carbonized by heating it until it turned to carbon was the best choice. When this thread was inserted into a glass bulb, and the air was pumped out, the filament glowed for 13 hours.

With more work, better bulbs were developed, and soon the Menlo Park laboratory was glowing with electric light bulbs. This did not completely solve the problem that Edison set out to solve, however. The world needed more than just an electric

light bulb. It needed a reliable system for getting the needed electricity to houses and businesses so they could use the light bulbs.

So Edison set his team to developing generators, wires, and cable. They also developed sockets, switches, fuses, lamp fixtures, and many other devices that were needed to make electric lights a reality in the home. It took two years of relentless work, but eventually the Menlo Park team had a working system. And in 1882 Edison set up the first commercially successful power station. Since that time, electric lighting and electric power in the home have become the standard that most Americans cannot imagine living without.

Today's light bulbs no longer use cotton thread fibers as the filament material. Instead, they use tungsten wire filaments. Tungsten lasts many times longer than carbonized thread. Also, the filament lasts much longer if the light bulb is filled with an inert gas instead of being a vacuum. **Inert gases** are elements that

Modern Conveniences

FINDING VARIOUS LIGHT BULBS

Be a light bulb detective. Search your house for as many different kinds of light bulbs as you can find. Test each bulb to see what color of light it produces and how bright it is. Some light bulbs produce a whiter light, while others are more yellow.

Flashlight bulbs are more directed than lamp bulbs. A 40-watt bulb will produce a dimmer light than a 60-watt bulb.

Count how many light bulbs are being used in each room of your house. Don't forget the light in the refrigerator, stove, microwave, or other unexpected places. How many light bulbs are in your house? Are you thankful for the electric light bulb?

do not easily react chemically. Most incandescent light bulbs are filled with argon or nitrogen gas because these gases do not easily react with tungsten.

An inert gas in the bulb helps the light bulb to last much longer. As the tungsten heats up, some of the tungsten atoms change from solid to a gas and float away from the filament. In a vacuum, these atoms hit the side of the bulb and stick there. Eventually one area of the filament will become too thin and will break apart, causing the bulb to "burn out." If the bulb is filled with an inert gas, the molecules of the gas help to reflect the tungsten atoms back toward the filament again where they cool down enough to become solid and reinforce the filament. Some of the atoms are still conducted away from the filament and stick to the top of the bulb. This is why you may see a dark circle at the end of a light bulb when you replace it. But the filament lasts much longer with the gas available to reflect the atoms back toward the filament than it does in a vacuum. ■

WHAT DID WE LEARN?

- What does incandescent mean?
- Why is it important that there be no oxygen inside a light bulb?
- Who is credited with inventing the first incandescent light bulb?

TAKING IT FURTHER

- How might a light bulb be designed to keep any stray oxygen atoms from burning up the filament?
- Premium light bulbs are filled with krypton instead of argon or nitrogen. Krypton is a heavier element than the other inert gases. How might krypton make the light bulb better?
- Some light bulbs claim to burn cooler than ordinary bulbs. Is this an advantage or disadvantage?
- Why do refrigerator light bulbs last so long?

ALTERNATIVE BULBS

Scientists and engineers are always looking for ways to make light bulbs more efficient and longer lasting. Several types of lighting are available today that are more efficient—that is they produce more light for a given amount of electricity—and are longer lasting than standard incandescent bulbs.

First, **halogen bulbs** (see photo below) produce a whiter light and last longer than standard incandescent bulbs. Halogen lights are incandescent bulbs, but they are not filled with an inert gas. Instead, they are filled with halogen gas, which reacts with the tungsten atoms when they evaporate. These molecules do not stick to the inside of the bulb. Instead, they fly around inside the bulb until they hit the filament. The heat from the filament breaks apart the molecules and redeposits the tungsten on the filament. This greatly increases the lifespan of the filament. Also, because the filament in a halogen light can burn hotter, it gives off more blue and less infrared light, so it has a whiter appearance and is more energy efficient. Many cars now have halogen headlights.

The second type of light that is more efficient than standard

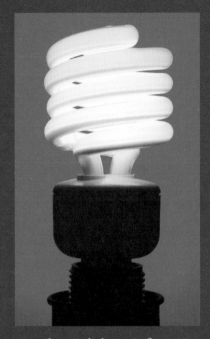

incandescent lighting is fluorescent lighting. **Fluorescent bulbs** contain a gas that becomes a plasma when current is passed through it. The plasma emits ultraviolet light. The inside of the bulb is coated with a phosphor coating that glows when it is hit by ultraviolet light. The word fluorescent comes from the element fluorite. Fluorite is a substance that glows under an ultraviolet light. Fluorescent lights are usually more efficient than incandescent bulbs, and because they do not have a filament that burns out, they last many times longer than ordinary light bulbs. Most of the time we think of fluorescent light bulbs as being long tubes, but many of the newer bulbs are coiled so that they take up about the same amount of

room as an incandescent bulb and can often be used in place of an ordinary bulb (see photo at left).

Light-emitting diodes, or LEDs, are the newest light bulb to replace incandescent bulbs. LEDs are tiny light bulbs that do not have a filament. Instead, they contain semiconducting material, often aluminum-gallium-arsenide, that glows when current passes through it. One or two tiny bulbs can replace the bulb in a flashlight (see photo below). These bulbs use a fraction of the energy that incandescent bulbs use and last many times longer. Several LEDs can be placed together to replace larger incandescent light bulbs. One popular use of LEDs is in traffic signals. LEDs do not have to be replaced as often and use only a small amount of the energy of the incandescent bulbs they replace. LEDs come in many colors and are even being used in strings of Christmas lights.

Questions: Why might someone choose to use halogen bulbs instead of incandescent bulbs? Why might someone choose to use fluorescent bulbs instead of incandescent bulbs?

THOMAS EDISON

1847–1931

"Genius is 1 percent inspiration and 99 percent perspiration"

Thomas Alva Edison was born in 1847, and is possibly the greatest inventor of all time. He was the youngest of seven children. This man who did so much to shape the path of technology was homeschooled by his loving mother. His mother, the daughter of a minister, pulled Thomas out of school within his first year, after the teacher said he was addled, or confused. He was described this way because Thomas wanted to know how things worked, so he asked too many questions. His father wanted him to learn about many different things, and paid him for every book he read. Thomas's first book was on science. Thomas used the money his father gave him to buy jars of chemicals which he labeled "POISON" to keep others from touching them. He used the chemicals to do experiments in his basement.

Thomas's father also wanted him to be outside more, so in the summer of 1858, young Tom along with a friend, planted a large vegetable garden and sold the produce. He made about $600.00 that year, but he didn't do this again as he did not like working in the hot sun. This was the same year that he became fascinated with the telegraph and built his own telegraph line. He ran a line between his home and a friend's house about ½ mile away.

The following year Thomas started working as a train boy selling newspapers and candy on the train that ran between his small town of Port Huron and Detroit. The train went to Detroit each morning and came back that evening. During his layover in Detroit, he would often spend his time at the library reading books, or he would stay on the train doing experiments in the baggage car where he had set up a small lab. When the Civil War started, Thomas saw that people along his route were very eager to receive news about the battles, so when the battle at Shiloh started he asked a telegraph operator in Detroit to send a message about the battle to the towns along his route. Then he bought 1,000 newspapers instead of his normal 100, and sold them on his way home, raising the price at each stop. About this time, he noticed that he was losing his hearing, but no one knows the exact reason why.

On one trip, some of his chemicals fell in the baggage car, starting a fire. The fire was put out, but Thomas lost his job on the train and could only sell his papers at the train stops. While at one of these train stations, he saved the life of a young boy who just happened to be the son of the station's telegraph operator. The grateful father offered to teach Thomas how to operate the telegraph, and Thomas eagerly accepted. He spent the next six years picking up work as a telegraph operator. Along the way, he experimented with ways to improve the telegraph. At one of his jobs he was working the night shift and had to send in a signal every half hour. He found this to be somewhat boring, so he used a small clock to send the signal so he could work on experiments or sleep. He was caught and told to stay awake.

Edison's first patent was for a vote recorder for Congress, which did not sell because the Congressmen wanted to cast their votes vocally so they could give short speeches with their votes. He resolved then to never again invent something that no one wanted. He started working on a duplex telegraph, one that could send two signals across the same wire. When he tried to demonstrate it, it didn't work. Discouraged, Thomas moved to New York with almost no money. A friend let him sleep in the S. S. Laws' Gold Indicator Company building. One day their ticker, a form of telegraph that sent the changing price of gold to brokers, stopped working. Thomas was there to fix it and received a job on the spot.

Soon after that, he and some friends started their own invention company. One of the first items they made was an improved ticker. A young woman named Mary Stilwell worked for Edison's company. He began to court her and married her on December 25, 1871. They had three children together. The first two children, a girl and a boy, were nicknamed Dot and Dash after the signals used over the telegraph. In 1876 Thomas moved his shop to Menlo Park, New Jersey where he built a two-story building filled with books, instruments, and chemicals. This is where most of his inventing work was done.

Thomas next conducted experiments with Alexander Graham Bell's invention, the telephone, and was able to improve it. From this work, he invented a device that would record and play back sounds. The phonograph worked the first time he tried it. Thomas demonstrated it to Congress and the president of the United States called Thomas the "Wizard of Menlo Park." Edison later miniaturized this invention placing it in a small doll.

Next, Edison turned his talent to another need—electric lights. During the late 19th century, homes used candles and gas lamps, both of which had many problems. Edison wanted to be the inventor of electric lights, but he also knew many others were working on it. So, in September 1878, he announced he was very close to developing the light bulb and would have it out in six weeks. Investors scrambled to set up the Edison Electric Light Company. But it wasn't until the following year that he was able to build a working light. His company then had to build all the other needed pieces, like switches and generators, in order to make it possible to use in homes. When he took the invention to France, Edison was awarded five gold medals and was made an officer in the French Legion of Honor.

Sadness hit in 1884 when his wife caught typhoid; Thomas stayed by her bed until she died. The following year he met Mina Miller and was immediately attracted. He taught her Morse code so they could send messages to each other even when others were around. Then one day he tapped out into her hand, "Will you marry me?" and she responded by tapping, "Yes." They were married and had three children together.

In 1928 Edison was awarded the Congressional Gold Medal for his many contributions to modern life. Thomas once said, "I never did anything worth doing by accident, nor did any of my inventions come by accident. They came by work." Thomas worked up to his death in October 1931. When he died, he had 1,093 patents in his name and the love of the world. He lay in state in the library of his West Orange laboratory for two days during which time 50,000 people filed by. Thomas Edison was a man who truly changed the world.

REFRIGERATION

Keeping things cool

LESSON

23

How do we keep our food cold?

Words to know:

heat

refrigeration

refrigerant

Imagine a hot summer day. You have been outside mowing the lawn or weeding the garden. You are hot and thirsty. You come into the kitchen and pour yourself a nice cool glass of water. You pull a few ice cubes out of the freezer to keep the water cold. Sounds great, right? You could not enjoy this refreshing drink if it were not for the invention of refrigeration. So what exactly is refrigeration?

To understand refrigeration, you must first understand heat. All objects have a certain amount of heat. **Heat** is energy that is contained in the movement of the molecules of the object. The more heat that is added to an object, the faster the molecules move and the higher the object's temperature becomes. Similarly, if heat is removed, the molecules slow down and the object's temperature goes down. With this in mind, it is important to think of **refrigeration** as the removal of heat, not the adding of cold since there is really no scientific definition of cold, only relative amounts of heat.

Refrigeration was invented primarily for preservation of food. We know that bacteria and molds can cause food to spoil and that bacteria and molds grow much more slowly in a cool environment; therefore, if we can keep foods in a cool place, they will spoil much more slowly.

Before we look at how a refrigerator works, we need to understand another important physical idea. Materials on earth exist in three basic states: solids, liquids, and gases. The state of an object depends on what material it is made out of and how much heat it has. For example, ice, water, and steam are all different states of a molecule containing two hydrogen atoms and one oxygen atom. When heat is added to water, its molecules begin to move faster. If enough heat is added, the water becomes steam. When a substance changes state, heat is either added or taken away

UNDERSTANDING REFRIGERATORS

The choice of which material to use as a refrigerant in your refrigerator is important. A substance can only absorb heat from an area that is warmer than it is, so the refrigerant must have a lower boiling point than 35°F (1.6°C) for the refrigerator or 32°F (0°C) for the freezer. This is why ammonia or HFCs are used. Their boiling points are significantly below 0°F (–18°C).

Purpose: To help understand how different substances can absorb different amounts of heat

Materials: glass of water, rubbing alcohol

Procedure:

1. Dip one finger into a glass of water then take it out. How does it feel compared to your other fingers? The wet finger will feel cooler than the dry fingers because heat is being pulled away from your finger as the water evaporates into the air, as it changes from a liquid into a gas.

2. Now, dip the same finger in the water again and dip a different finger into a dish of rubbing alcohol.

3. Take both fingers out of the liquids. Which finger feels cooler? The finger dipped in alcohol should feel cooler. Why?

Conclusion: The alcohol absorbs heat more quickly and turns to gas more quickly than the water, so it makes your finger feel cooler as it pulls the heat away faster than the water does.

Purpose: To understand the importance of insulation

Materials: two ice cubes, plate, washcloth, rubber band

Procedure:

1. Take two ice cubes that are approximately the same size. Place one ice cube on a plate and wrap the other ice cube in a thick washcloth and secure it with a rubber band.

2. Place the wrapped ice cube next to the plate.

3. Time how long it takes for the first ice cube to melt completely.

4. As soon as it has completely melted, open the wash cloth and observe the second ice cube. How does the second ice cube compare to the first? It has probably melted only a small amount because the

wash cloth kept most of the heat away from the ice cube.

Conclusion: Refrigerators are designed to keep foods cool by taking heat away from the inside of the box. However, keeping heat out to begin with is also important. The walls of your refrigerator are filled with insulating materials. Insulators do not easily allow heat to pass through. Thus, the insulated walls help to keep the heat out.

---

from the substance. When changing from solid to liquid, or from liquid to gas, heat must be added to the substance. When changing the other direction, either from gas to liquid or liquid to solid, heat must be removed from the substance. This is the basis for refrigeration. A substance must experience a change of state so that heat can be transferred.

You want the inside of your refrigerator to remain between 35°F and 38°F (1.6°C–3.3°C) to keep your food fresh. But warmer air quickly enters your refrigerator when you open the door, and heat also slowly seeps in around the seal of the door. So you need to remove this excess heat to keep the food from spoiling. This is done through a mechanical process that causes substances to change state.

Some commercial refrigeration systems use ammonia as the refrigerant, the substance that changes state. Ammonia is used because it boils at –27°F. However, ammonia gas can be toxic, so most home refrigerators do not use it. From the 1930s to the 1970s, chlorofluorocarbons (CFCs) were used as the refrigerant, but in the 1970s it was discovered that CFCs may harm the ozone layer in the atmosphere. So

Modern Conveniences

today, HFCs, or hydrofluorocarbons, are used as the refrigerant in home refrigerators.

Let's look at how a refrigerator actually works. In the back of your refrigerator, behind the area where you store the food, is a series of pipes and other equipment which do the real work to keep your food cold. To begin with, liquid refrigerant is under pressure. This liquid flows through a valve, called an expansion valve, into pipes where the pressure is lower. As the liquid expands, it turns into a gas. In order for the liquid to change to a gas it must absorb heat. This heat comes from the inside of your refrigerator as the air from the refrigerator moves around the pipes. Thus, the temperature inside the refrigerator is lowered.

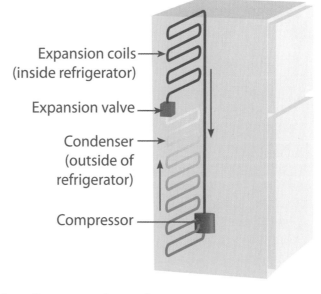

Expansion coils (inside refrigerator)

Expansion valve

Condenser (outside of refrigerator)

Compressor

FUN FACT

The same process that cools the inside of your refrigerator is also used by air conditioning units to cool down the inside of your home or office. Because a building is much larger than a refrigerator, a much larger compressor is needed, but the process is the same.

But the job cannot end there. The refrigerant must be recycled so it can be used again. Thus, the gas flows into a compressor that applies pressure to the gas. This changes the gas back into a liquid. Remember, when a gas changes back into a liquid, it releases heat. We don't want that heat to go back inside the refrigerator, so the liquid flows through some pipes called the condenser that are located on the outside of the refrigerator, where the released heat can move into the air in your kitchen. Most refrigerators have a fan that blows air across these pipes to help move the heat into the air. If you stand near your refrigerator, you will probably feel warm air either coming out the bottom below the door, or out from behind the refrigerator. ■

WHAT DID WE LEARN?

- What is refrigeration?
- What is the ideal temperature for the inside of a refrigerator?
- Why is this the ideal temperature range?
- What substance is used as a refrigerant in most new refrigerators?

TAKING IT FURTHER

- Can you cool your kitchen by leaving the refrigerator door open? Why or why not?
- What is the best way to make your refrigerator more efficient?
- When you open the refrigerator door, some moisture from the air condenses on the evaporation, or expansion, coils. How might you stop a buildup of ice from becoming a problem?
- How does a refrigerator keep the inside from becoming too cold?

CHEMICAL REFRIGERATORS

Modern Conveniences

The type of refrigerator described on the previous page is a mechanical refrigerator, which uses compression and expansion to help the refrigerant change phases. However, there are other types of refrigerators.

Most recreational vehicles use a propane gas-powered refrigerator. This type of refrigerator uses chemical reactions to cause the necessary phase changes. First, we start with liquid ammonia. This liquid combines with hydrogen, which causes it to evaporate. This evaporation requires heat and thus removes heat from the interior of the refrigerator. The gas then flows into an absorber, which contains water. The ammonia combines with the water and releases the hydrogen. Next, the ammonia and water enter a generator that is heated by burning propane. The heat from the propane causes the ammonia and water to boil. The gases then flow into a separator where the ammonia is separated from the water. The ammonia gas then flows into a condenser where it becomes a liquid, thus releasing the heat that was added to it. From there, the ammonia flows to the evaporator where it again mixes with the hydrogen and the process is repeated.

The phase changes are still the main method of removing heat from the refrigerator, but this process does not use a mechanical compressor to bring about those phase changes.

Questions: Why do you think an RV is built with a propane refrigerator? How are chemical refrigerators similar to mechanical refrigerators? How are they different?

Most RVs have a chemical refrigerator.

FREDERICK MCKINLEY JONES

1892–1961

red Jones was the son of a red-haired Irishman and an African American woman. Fred was born on May 17, 1892 or 1893, in Covington, Kentucky. His mother died when he was very young and his father, John, was a laborer for the railroads. His father knew that Fred was very smart. Fred was always taking things apart to see how they worked. John's job required him to move to wherever the railroad needed him, but he wanted his son to get a good education, so when Fred was seven his father sent him to live and be educated at a local Catholic church in Cincinnati, Ohio. After Fred's father spoke with the priest, he said goodbye to his son, saying he would come back to get him when he could. That was the last time Fred ever saw his father; he died when Fred was nine.

Fred stayed at the Catholic school until he was twelve, attending classes and working around the church to earn his keep. One Saturday Fred went with a friend to Crother's Garage. Fred was fascinated. Here in one location was everything he had always dreamed of—cars, engines, motors, and tools. He decided to run away from the school and went to Crother's Garage. He told Mr. Crother that he was fourteen and he begged for a job. He was big for

his age so Mr. Crother believed him and hired him to sweep the floors. He learned everything he could by watching and reading the manuals and by the time he was really fourteen he was a full-time mechanic. By the time he was fifteen he was the foreman. Even though Fred could build and fix the race cars, his boss did not want him at the racetracks. However, one day he went to see the cars. This made Mr. Crother angry and the next day he told Fred to take a vacation without pay. So he did.

Fred went south but found he was not accepted in the south. The white people would not let him work on their cars and the black people looked at him as haughty. He was unable to find work so he headed back north to Chicago. Chicago was only a little better for him. When winter came, Fred found himself hungry with only short-term work. So he jumped a train and ended up in Effingham, Illinois where he found work fixing the furnace and other parts of an old hotel. When the owner of the hotel sold it, he asked Fred to come work on his new farm. In the nearby town, Fred was accepted by most of the people and made several friends. He again gained a reputation as the man who could fix anything. His job lasted until the owner of the farm died.

Fred enlisted in the army during World War I. When his commander learned that Fred understood electricity, he had Fred rewire the camps in the area along with keeping the telephone and telegraph working. After returning home, he built a snow sled for his friend, a doctor, to help him get around in the winter. Fred sometimes helped the doctors in the area by keeping their equipment running. He installed the first X-ray machine in town. There was a need for a portable X-ray machine, so he studied more and built one, but he never considered patenting this idea.

In 1920 Fred became interested in moving pictures. The new owners of the local theater needed his help. Their equipment was old but they wanted to be able to show talking pictures. Fred built a record player for them that kept time with the movie. Later, Hollywood started putting the sound on the film. Fred studied optics and built a special lens to focus the light so the old projector could use the new film. The sound machine he built was the best in the area and salesmen would plan their trips to end up in his town on the weekends so they could go to the movies.

Word of Fred's talent got around and he received job offers from companies as far away as Minneapolis. His friends told him he should give it a try. If it didn't work out he could always come back. On his way out of town, Fred stopped in at the Ultraphone Sound System Company and never left. The owner, Joseph Numero, saw what Fred could do, so he offered Fred an apartment and a small salary and gave him a place to work with all the equipment he needed. In exchange, everything Fred invented would belong to the company. Fred helped Ultraphone Sound System put out some of the best sound equipment in the industry.

One day in 1939, Joe, Fred's boss, was playing golf with some friends when one of the men complained that one of his trucks had broken down and his truckload of food had spoiled. He asked his friends why someone couldn't come up with a cooler for trucks. He was told that the equipment only worked in a stationary location; as soon as the refrigerator was put on a truck the movement would knock the whole thing apart. Joe, however, said that Fred could do it. The next Monday, Harry Werner called Joe and told him he had just bought a 24′ trailer for him to put the refrigerator on. So Fred was given a real challenge.

Once delivered, Fred looked the trailer over for about 30 minutes, then turned to Joe and said he thought he could come up with something. His first design weighed 2,200 pounds and went under the trailer. When he tried it out, it didn't work as well as he hoped so he redesigned it to work better and made it 400 pounds lighter. The refrigerated truck was such a success that Joe sold the sound company and went into the business of building refrigerated trucks. Refrigerated trucks allowed food to be moved all over the country without going bad. This started a whole new industry; small corner grocery stores became supermarkets, and people could eat fresh fruits and vegetables year round.

Fred went on to redesign the units to ride above the truck cab and to weigh only 950 pounds. When World War II started, the military asked Fred to design a small portable refrigeration unit that could be used by field hospitals. Again, Fred was able to come up with a design that worked. In 1945, Fred met and later married Louise Lucille Powell. Fred earned 90 patents, 60 for refrigeration alone, but never earned much money. Money was not important to him. He had what he needed—a loving wife, a home to live in, clothes, food, and a place to experiment in. Fred died from lung cancer in 1961, at the age of 68, after revolutionizing the refrigeration industry.

SEWING MACHINE

The treadle

How does a sewing machine work?

Words to know:

treadle

Challenge words:

shuttle

Modern Conveniences

Since Adam and Eve first ate the forbidden fruit in the Garden of Eden (Genesis 3), people have been making clothing. How these clothes have been sewn together has varied from one culture to another, but most clothing has been sewn using a needle and some kind of thread. With the advent of the Industrial Revolution, the clothing industry was one of the first to change. The steam engine was used to power looms so that weaving cloth became much easier and faster. However, sewing that cloth into shirts, pants, and dresses remained a very labor-intensive job as each seam had to be done by hand.

Many people in several countries were trying to develop a sewing machine at about the same time. In 1830 a Frenchman named Barthélemy Thimonnier developed a sewing machine that did embroidery and regular stitching. He used his machines to sew uniforms for the French soldiers. However, he experienced great opposition from the tailors in his town who broke in and destroyed most of his machines. Later, Thimonnier was caught in the violence of the French Revolution and fled to England and then to the United States. He was not successful in marketing his invention in either of those countries.

Between 1832 and 1834 an American named Walter Hunt invented a sewing machine that used many of the ideas still employed in today's machines. Hunt's machine had a needle with the eye at the bottom instead of at the top. It also used two different threads and a shuttle for making the seams. These advancements were very important for making a successful sewing machine. Hunt developed his machine, but when his daughter pointed out how many seamstresses would be put out of business by his invention, he decided not to patent his invention.

In 1845 another American, Elias Howe Jr., made the first successful sewing machine. He patented his invention in 1846. It is unclear if Howe made his invention completely independently, or if he used some of Hunt's design, but his final design had many of the features found in Hunt's sewing machine.

One of the most important steps in developing a sewing machine was changing the way we think about sewing. When a person sews by hand, the eye of the needle which holds the thread is at the top, so the needle must pass completely through the fabric in order for the thread to go through the fabric. Many of the early sewing machines tried to imitate hand sewing, but they were not successful. Once people realized that sewing could be accomplished in a different way with a machine than it was done by hand, many advancements were made. Often, inventions result when someone is able to view a problem from a different perspective. The first big advancement in sewing machine design was to place the eye of the needle near the bottom so the needle only had to go a small distance into the fabric. Other ideas quickly followed.

One person to make significant improvements to Howe's design was Isaac Merritt Singer. Singer worked in a machine shop and one day a sewing machine came in for repair. After working on the machine, Singer decided he could make significant improvements to the design, which he did. Howe's machine moved the fabric vertically, but Singer's machine moved it horizontally, allowing for faster sewing. Also, sewing machines were hand-powered by turning a wheel while sewing. But Singer invented the treadle, which was a foot operated device to turn the wheels, thus freeing up the seamstresses' hands to control the fabric. Singer also designed a presser foot that held the fabric in place while it was being sewn and a wheel that pushed the fabric through the machine. These were very important improvements. Singer sewing machines were some of the most popular, and even today when people think of sewing machines, they often associate them with the name Singer.

FUN FACT

- In 1863 the sewing machine could sew 500 stitches per minute while the average seamstress could sew 30 stitches per minute.
- By 1882 sewing machines could sew 68 different kinds of stitches.
- By 1900 there were over 125 sewing machine companies in the United States.
- Singer made the sewing machine affordable for many people by offering a payment plan that allowed families to pay in monthly installments.

EXAMINING A SEWING MACHINE

Purpose: To see how modern sewing machines are marvelous time savers

Materials: cloth, sewing machine, needle and thread

Activity 1—Procedure:

With adult supervision, examine how a sewing machine does each of the following:

1. Hold the cloth in place
2. Feed the cloth through as it is being sewn
3. Feed the thread through the needle
4. Take the thread through the cloth and hold it in place
5. Make repeated stitches

Activity 2—Procedure:

1. Cut four squares of cloth 4 inches on each side.
2. Using a sewing needle and thread, stitch two pieces of cloth together by hand.
3. Now, sew the other two pieces of cloth together using a sewing machine. Which was easier? Which looks better?

Aren't you glad for the invention of the sewing machine?

The sewing machine got off to a rather slow start, but when the Civil War started, the demand for uniforms, blankets, and other supplies greatly increased the demand for sewing machines. In 1890 electric motors were added to machines to replace the treadle that had been used. Sewing machine technology has kept pace with other technologies, and today's machines have computer controls that make different kinds of stitches at the press of a button. Also, overlocking machines, or sergers, have been developed which use three or four threads instead of just two to give seams a finished look.

And what about Hunt's fear that the sewing machine would put women out of work? Because machine-sewn clothing was much less expensive, the demand for manufactured clothing greatly increased, so the need for seamstresses actually went up. ■

An industrial overlock machine

Modern Conveniences

WHAT DID WE LEARN?

- What are some of the problems that had to be solved before a useful sewing machine could be built?
- What were some improvements made by Isaac Singer?

TAKING IT FURTHER

- How is sewing with a machine similar to sewing by hand?
- How is sewing with a machine different from sewing by hand?
- How did the Civil War affect the demand for sewing machines?

SECURING STITCHES

The key to a mechanical sewing machine was discovering a way to secure the stitches. When sewing by hand the needle draws the thread completely through the fabric, but this was not practical for a machine. So an idea was taken from the loom. In a loom, vertical threads are set up in columns on the loom. Then a horizontal thread is carried across the vertical threads by a shuttle. The idea of a **shuttle** that could carry the thread through a second thread was the idea that made

sewing machines possible. The pictures below demonstrate how this works.

The top thread is taken through the fabric by the needle. Underneath the fabric is a bobbin that contains a second thread. A shuttle that rotates around the bobbin catches a loop of the top thread as the needle comes down. The shuttle then rotates, carrying the loop with it. Part of the loop passes in front of the bobbin and part of the loop passes behind the bobbin. The shuttle then carries

the loop through a loop of the bobbin thread. As the needle pulls up, the top thread is pulled tight and the bobbin thread holds the stitch in place.

Open up your sewing machine and observe the actions of the shuttle and needle as you slowly turn the wheel of the machine. Note how the top thread is passed through the bobbin thread to create a stitch. If you have access to a serger, or overlocking machine, see if you can figure out how the stitches are secured on that machine.

MODERN APPLIANCES

What's in your house

LESSON 25

How do modern appliances save us work?

Words to know:

thermostat

microwave

agitator

What would our lives be like without all of the appliances in our homes? A hundred years ago many hours each day were devoted to washing clothes, cleaning house, cooking, and sewing. Today, only a small fraction of our time is spent doing these activities. Why? Because of the discovery of electricity and the subsequent invention of all the labor-saving devices that have been developed that use electricity. Thomas Edison worked to bring electricity to people's homes so they could use electric lights, but the ready availability of electricity also made electrical appliances practical.

Most American homes are filled with these devices. From toasters to washing machines, appliances save us time and effort in many ways. We cannot discuss every appliance in one lesson, but we will discuss a few of the most common appliances found in many homes.

Cooking is an important part of everyone's life. Whether you personally prepare the meals, or just eat them, it is important to have a way to cook your food. Although stoves and ovens have always been used in one capacity or another, modern stoves are much safer and more convenient than stoves of the past. Many homes have an electric stove and oven. In an electric stove, electricity is passed through heating coils that glow red as they heat up. The heat is then passed from the stove to the pan and from the pan to the food. Similarly, inside an oven, electricity is passed through a heating coil and the heat is transferred to the air

inside the oven. The heat then moves from the air into the pan and then to the food. Inside the oven, a thermostat is used to measure the temperature and control the flow of electricity to keep the temperature in the oven within an acceptable range.

In 1945 a new type of oven was invented. Percy Spencer invented the microwave oven to cook popcorn. The microwave oven works very differently from an electric or gas oven. Instead of heating the area around the food, a microwave oven works directly on the food itself. Microwaves, which are waves of energy, are generated inside the oven. As these energy waves pass through the food, they excite the water molecules causing them to vibrate. As molecules move faster, their temperature goes up. This is a more efficient way to heat food, so microwave ovens generally cook food in less time than other ovens. Interestingly, today one of the most popular foods to cook in a microwave oven is microwave popcorn.

Another important time-saving device found in most homes is the vacuum cleaner. When houses primarily had floors without carpet, it was fairly easy to get rid of the dirt and dust by sweeping the floors and shaking or beating the rugs that were on top. However, with the increased use of permanent wall-to-wall carpeting, a better method was needed to clean floors. The vacuum cleaner was invented in 1902 by an American named Hubert Booth. Most vacuum cleaners have a rolling brush on the bottom that helps to sweep up the dirt and other particles from the top of the carpet as well as a suction fan powered by an electric motor. The dust is sucked into a bag or other container and stored for later disposal. Some vacuum cleaners also have air filters to help filter out particles that are stirred up by the vacuuming process.

One final device that saves many hours of labor is the clothes washing machine. In order to get dirt out of clothing, it is necessary for detergent and water to be passed through the cloth several times with some force. In the past, people used rocks or scrubbing boards to get dirt out of their clothing, but during the Industrial Revolution many people worked on developing a machine that could do this job. In the 1920s a semi-automatic machine was designed, but it wasn't until 1937 that the first fully-automatic washing machine was built. In a washing machine, clothes are placed in a tub that contains an agitator, which is a device with fins to help move the clothing. In some machines, the agitator moves, in others the tub moves back and forth. Either way, the clothes are pushed through the water and detergent to help get out the dirt. Electric motors and gear mechanisms control the movement of the agitator and tub. When the washing cycle is completed, the tub spins and water is removed from the clothes. After the rinse cycle, the clothes can then be hung on a line to dry or placed in a clothes dryer. Some washing machines can dry the clothes as well, but most machines only do the washing.

You can probably find tens or even dozens of labor-saving devices in your home if you look. Be thankful that God gave people the ingenuity to design these devices so you can have more time for learning, exercising, helping others, and playing. ■

THE USE OF CENTRIPETAL FORCE

A washing machine spins most of the water out of the clothes at the end of the washing and rinse cycles. This works because of centripetal and centrifugal forces. According to Newton's first law of motion, a moving body travels along a straight path with constant speed (i.e., has constant velocity) unless it is acted on by an outside force. The spinning tub exerts a centripetal force on the clothes and keeps them moving in a circle. When the tub pushes on the clothes, the clothes push back. As the clothes push up against the side of the tub water is squeezed out of them. The tub has holes in it so the water keeps moving outward through the holes.

Purpose: To see how centripetal force works in a washer tub

Materials: washcloth, net bag, string, measuring cup, dish, plastic bag

Procedure:

1. Place a washcloth in a net bag and tie the end shut with a piece of string.

2. Pour one cup of water into a 2-cup measuring cup.

3. Dip the bag with the washcloth into the measuring cup until the cloth is completely soaked and pour out any remaining water.

4. Hang the bag by the string over an empty dish for thirty minutes.

5. Next, place the net bag and washcloth inside a larger plastic bag.

6. Securely tie the end of the plastic bag around the end of the net bag with another piece of string, as shown here.

7. Take the bags outside to an empty area and swing the bags by the string in a circle for 2 minutes.

8. Carefully remove the net bag from the plastic bag without letting the washcloth touch the water in the bottom of the bag.

9. Pour the water from the plastic bag into the measuring cup to see how much water you were able to spin out of the washcloth. The net bag acts like the tub of the washer, keeping the washcloth inside the bag, but allowing the water to leave.

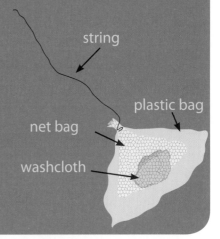

string

plastic bag

net bag

washcloth

WHAT DID WE LEARN?

- What is the purpose of an electrical appliance?

- What are some of the major appliances in your home?

- Explain how one of these devices saves you time and effort.

TAKING IT FURTHER

- If you were to invent a new appliance what would it be and how would it work?

TIME-SAVERS

Your home is probably filled with electrical appliances. Complete the "Household Appliances" worksheet to get an idea of how much time you save by using these appliances.

Clocks

What time is it?

LESSON

26

Modern Conveniences

How have clocks changed over the years?

Words to know:

chronometer

crystal oscillator

What time is it? How many times a day do you ask that question? Time is something that everyone has to spend. God has given each of us 24 hours a day and we must use our time wisely. Man has always understood that time is important. Even ancient civilizations tried to find ways to keep track of time. The ancient Egyptians built huge obelisks that served as giant sundials. The Romans made the sundial more useful by making it smaller and more precise. This was the main way of telling time for many centuries.

In the 800s English monks used candles as clocks. The candles were a specific height and thickness so they would burn at a known rate. The sides of the candles were marked so it was possible to tell how long the candle had been burning. Then in the 1300s glass making advanced and hour glasses or sand clocks were developed. At about this same time weighted clocks were developed. A weighted clock has a weight suspended on a rope. The rope was wound around a drum. As the weight was pulled down by gravity, the drum turned and moved the gears of the clock.

All of these devices were somewhat helpful in keeping track of time, but none was very accurate. The real breakthrough in clock technology came when Galileo discovered the properties of pendulums around 1630. Galileo discovered that a pendulum swings at the same rate regardless of how wide its arc is. He also discovered that the weight of the pendulum did not affect its rate. The only

characteristic that affects the rate at which the pendulum swings is the length of the pendulum. This was a great discovery because this meant that a pendulum of the right length could be used to accurately keep time.

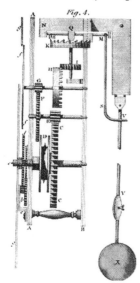

Huygens clock

Although Galileo made this discovery, he did not actually build an accurate pendulum clock. The man to do that was Christian Huygens. Huygens was an astronomer who needed an accurate time piece for the measurements he wanted to make, so in 1657 he developed the first accurate pendulum clock. In a pendulum clock, the pendulum swings at a set rate and moves a rocker arm with each swing. The rocker arm allows an escape wheel to move one notch. This wheel turns the drive wheel which in turn moves gears that move the minute and hour hands. The differences in the gears allow the minute hand to move at a different rate than the hour hand, but the steady rate of the pendulum keeps everything moving at a specified rate.

An accurate clock was useful in a multitude of ways. Navigation was one area where an accurate clock was badly needed. For centuries sailors had been using the stars to help them determine latitude—how far north or south they were. But the stars could not help a sailor determine how far east or west he was. An accurate clock was needed for that. In 1736, an English clockmaker named John Harrison designed a chronometer—a clock used for navigation. It was tested and although it was more accurate than other clocks, it was not accurate enough. So Harrison improved the design, and in 1741 he built a chronometer that was accurate enough for determining longitude. This invention is credited with saving many sailors' lives, since they could now know exactly where they were, even when not in sight of land.

Clockmakers have continued to improve clocks, finding ways to overcome friction and errors due to changes in temperature, so today's clocks are extremely accurate. Today, many clocks are still powered mechanically. Mechanical clocks have a spring or other device that is wound up and slowly releases the power. However, most clocks and watches made today are driven by electricity in the form of a small battery. Current from the battery passes through a quartz crystal oscillator. The oscillator vibrates and produces electrical pulses at a very precise rate. These pulses go through a microchip which slows the pulses down to 1 pulse per second. These pulses power an electromagnet that in turn moves a drive wheel that turns the hands on the clock. In the case of

rocker arm

escape wheel

pendulum

FUN FACT

The most accurate clocks today are atomic clocks. Atomic clocks use the vibrations of cesium atoms to mark the time. These atoms vibrate at a very specific frequency. The atomic clock is the benchmark for time worldwide and is broadcast via satellite for agencies to use to set their own clocks.

MARKING TIME

Purpose: To make a simple pendulum clock

Materials: metal washer or nut, string, stopwatch

Procedure:

1. Tie a weight such as a metal washer or nut to the end of a piece of string.

2. Tape the other end of the string to the edge of a table.

3. Use a stopwatch to measure how long it takes for the pendulum to make one complete swing back and forth.

4. Adjust the length of the pendulum until the time for the swing is exactly 1 second.

Conclusion: Now you have a simple clock to measure seconds. Use your clock to measure various things like how long you can stand on one foot, how long you can hold your breath, or how many times your heart beats in fifteen seconds.

FUN FACT

All clocks need a power source, but some watches have what may be an unexpected source—you. Some watches use the regular movements of your body to help wind a spring or power a small generator so that you do not need to wind the watch or replace a battery.

digital clocks or watches, these pulses drive an integrated circuit which displays the time on a liquid crystal display (LCD).

Accurate clocks and watches are an everyday part of our lives. They help us be on time to church and catch our planes, but they do not give us any more time. We still have to be wise stewards of God's precious resources. ■

WHAT DID WE LEARN?

- What is a clock?
- What is the main difference between a mechanical clock and an electric clock?
- Why was a pendulum an important part of an accurate clock?

TAKING IT FURTHER

- Why was an accurate clock so necessary for navigation?
- Other than navigation, name two areas where accurate clocks are needed.

WATER CLOCKS

Records show that as far back as 2000 BC, the Egyptians made water clocks to help them keep track of time, and about AD 800 the Arabs were building very elaborate water clocks. But what exactly is a water clock? A water clock is a container filled with water that has a hole that allows the water to flow out. The level of the water indicates how much time has passed.

Purpose: To experiment with some simple water clocks

Materials: two half-gallon milk cartons, nail, modeling clay, 2-liter soda bottle, straw, masking tape, stopwatch, "Water Clocks" work-sheet

Procedure:

1. Use a nail to punch a hole in the bottom of one half-gallon milk carton and the side of the other carton as pictured above.

2. Plug both holes with modeling clay and fill both cartons with water.

3. Hold each carton over the sink with the hole pointing down and remove the clay from both holes at the same time.

4. Use a stopwatch to record how long it takes for the water to flow out of each carton. Record your measurements on a copy of the "Water Clocks" worksheet.

5. Now let's make a water clock where we can see the level of the water. Cut the bottom off a 2-liter soda bottle.

6. Plug the neck of the bottle with modeling clay and insert a soda straw through the clay and then remove any clay that is stuck inside the straw.

7. Place your finger over the end of the straw, hold the bottle over a bucket, and fill the bottle with water.

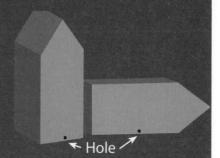

← Hole →

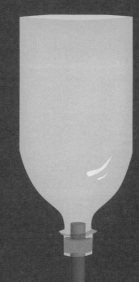

8. Remove your finger and observe the flow of the water from the bottle. Does the water flow at a continuous rate? Why not?

9. Place a strip of masking tape along the side of the bottle.

10. Refill the bottle with water and begin a timer when the water starts flowing.

11. Use a marker to mark the water level in the bottle after each minute (or 15 seconds if the bottle empties quickly). Now you have a simple water clock.

12. Write your observations on your worksheet and answer the rest of the questions.

UNIT

5

MEDICAL INVENTIONS

MICROSCOPE

Opening up a whole new world

How can we see very small things?

Words to know:

simple microscope

compound microscope

objective

eyepiece

achromatic

electron microscope

scanning tunneling microscope/STM

Technological advances in medicine have saved millions of lives. Today, doctors can diagnose and treat hundreds of conditions that were deadly only a hundred and fifty years ago. We could not possibly list all the advances that have contributed to medical science, but we will examine a few. A couple of simple inventions that are important to medicine include the stethoscope and the syringe. A French doctor named René Laennec invented the stethoscope in 1819. Laennec felt it was inappropriate to place his ear against a woman's chest to listen to her heartbeat, so he rolled up a piece of paper and listened through it. He noticed that the sound was louder through the rolled paper, so he created a tube to amplify a patient's heartbeat. The design was improved in 1855 to include two separate earpieces. Another simple invention, the syringe with a hollow needle, was first used for giving injections by a French surgeon named Charles Gabriel Pravaz in 1850. A third invention, the thermometer, was also important to medicine. The thermometer was first used with the Fahrenheit scale around 1724 and is instrumental in detecting illness. Although these simple inventions are important, their contribution to medical advancement pales when compared to the invention of the microscope.

It is unclear who invented the first microscope, but we know it was invented around 1650. One of the first scientists to use the microscope was a

Medical Inventions

Dutchman named Anton Van Leeuwenhoek. Van Leeuwenhoek taught himself to grind lenses and used his lenses to build his own microscopes. His microscopes could enlarge objects up to 270 times. Van Leeuwenhoek is believed to be the first scientist to observe bacteria as well as many other microscopic organisms. This discovery began to open up the doors to understanding the human body and how it is affected by organisms that we cannot ordinarily see.

The earliest microscopes were simple microscopes with only one lens, but people quickly developed compound microscopes that had two lenses. In a compound microscope, the first or bottom lens, called the objective, enlarges the object. The second or top lens, called the eyepiece, magnifies the enlarged image, thus multiplying the magnification of the one lens by the magnification of the other.

The early microscopes had two main problems. First, there was a limit to how much they could magnify an image, and second, the lenses caused distortion. Sometime between 1820 and 1840 the achromatic microscope was developed. This microscope used a new lens that eliminated much of the distortion and could thus be made much stronger. For nearly a hundred years this was the best type of microscope available. This new microscope gave birth to the field of bacteriology and germ theory. Once scientists could see some of the organisms in the air and in the water, and when they could see the effects of these organisms on cells, they were able to begin making tremendous advancements in treating people.

All optical microscopes operate by passing light through a curved piece of glass called a lens. Because light bends as it travels from one medium to another, this allows an image to be magnified. However, it was discovered that there are limits to how much you can enlarge an image with lenses. Optical microscopes cannot show us anything smaller than the wavelength of light, so they can only enlarge objects a maximum of about 2,000 times. But a new way of enlarging objects was developed in 1933.

LEARNING ABOUT MICROSCOPES

Every scientist, regardless of his or her field of interest, will probably use an optical microscope at one time or another. So it is important to know what the parts of the microscope are and what they do. The base of the microscope supports the rest of the device. The stage is where the specimen is placed for observation. Below the stage is a light source. The light is usually a light bulb, but sometimes it is a mirror that reflects other light.

Often the stage has clips for holding the slide in place.

The light passes through the specimen into the lens of the objective. Most microscopes have more than one objective so the specimen can be viewed at different levels of magnification. On the side of the body are adjustment knobs that either move the stage up and down or move the objective up and down for focusing. Most microscopes have a coarse adjustment and a fine adjustment. The coarse adjustment

is usually a lager knob than the fine adjustment.

After light passes through the objective, it moves up the tube to the eyepiece, which contains a second lens. The objective magnifies the image perhaps 15 to 50 times. Then the eyepiece magnifies the magnified image perhaps another 10 times so the viewed image is actually 150 to 500 times the actual size. Complete the "Parts of a Microscope" worksheet to review the parts described above.

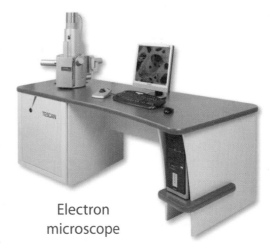

Electron microscope

In the 1920s Ernst Rusk, a German scientist, discovered that a magnetic coil could be used as a lens for electrons that bounced off of an object that was bombarded by a beam of electrons. He also discovered that two coils together would magnify the image just like when two optical lenses are used together. He worked on improving his design and in 1933 he developed the first electron microscope. An electron microscope can be used to view images that are much smaller than what can be seen with an optical microscope, enlarging objects up to a million times. This invention was even more useful for the medical world than the optical microscope. It has led to many discoveries in the area of bacteriology and enabled doctors to better fight disease.

More recently, in 1981, a new kind of microscope was developed by Gerd Binnig and Heinrich Rohrer that allows scientists to view even smaller objects. This new microscope is called a scanning tunneling microscope, or STM. The STM does not actually give a visual image of the object, but rather it sends electrical signals that are translated into a visual image by a computer and displayed on a screen. A stylus that is only one atom wide scans across the surface of an atom or molecule and the electrical current that passes between the stylus and the surface changes with the distance from the surface. This process is a little like a person reading Braille. The current is translated into a topographical map of the scanned surface. This discovery holds more potential for chemists and physicists than for medical researchers, but is important nevertheless. The 1986 Nobel Prize for physics was split between Rusk, Binnig, and Rohrer for their work in developing such amazing microscopes. ∎

WHAT DID WE LEARN?

- What is a microscope?
- How is a simple microscope different from a compound microscope?
- How did the achromatic lens improve the microscope?
- Name three simple medical inventions that are still used today.

TAKING IT FURTHER

- If you wanted to view viruses, would you use an optical or electron microscope?
- When might a simple microscope be better than a compound microscope?

RESEARCH PROJECT

Do some research on one of the following topics. Write a short paper and share it with your class or family: • Scanning electron microscope • Louis Pasteur • Bacteria and viruses • Joseph Lister

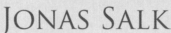

JONAS SALK

1914–1995

"It is courage based on confidence, not daring, and it is confidence based on experience."

How do you stop something that no one has seen but is harming millions of people? That was the problem during the first half of the 1900s, and it was called polio. No one knows how many people were affected, but in 1916, in New York City alone, there were 9,000 cases, mostly affecting children. In 1921 future President Franklin D. Roosevelt contracted polio and was left with severe paralysis. People were afraid to let their children go out in public places like swimming pools or schools. Polio was a killer, but help would someday be found.

In 1914 Jonas Salk was born to two Russian-Jewish immigrants who themselves lacked formal education, but were determined to see their children succeed. They encouraged their children to study, and study Jonas did. He was able to enter an accelerated high school program where he graduated at the age of fourteen. He received a full academic scholarship to the City College of New York. Jonas planned to pursue a law degree, but when he graduated in 1934, he had changed his plans and decided to become a doctor. He went to the New York University School of Medicine and graduated in 1939. He was married the next day to Donna Lindsay.

Salk worked for a few months for Dr. Thomas Francis, a professor at NYU Medical School in the field of microbiology, and then began his internship at Mount Sinai Hospital. The United States joined the Second World War in 1941, and in 1942 Jonas received a message from the draft board. He could either join the military or get a job researching something important to national defense. He contacted his old teacher, Dr. Francis, who now worked for the University of Michigan in the school of Public Health, and together they worked on a vaccine against the flu. In 1943 they had produced a vaccine that when tested on soldiers proved to be 75% successful, meaning that of the soldiers who received the vaccine, 75% fewer caught the flu compared to those who received a shot with no vaccine in it.

In 1947 Salk accepted an appointment to the University of Pittsburgh Medical School. He felt the same principles that he applied to the flu virus could be applied to a polio virus, and he worked on a vaccine for the next eight years. On April 12, 1955 he made the news public—he had a vaccine. The initial recipients included 1,830,000 children and the vaccine was shown to be safe and very effective. Salk refused to patent the vaccine and had no desire to profit from it. He wanted it to be used as widely as possible. However, he did receive the Congressional Gold Medal. Today, because of his work, polio is almost wiped out around the world. In 1963 Salk started his own research lab in La Jolla, California where he continued to work on other viruses until he died in 1995, at the age of 80.

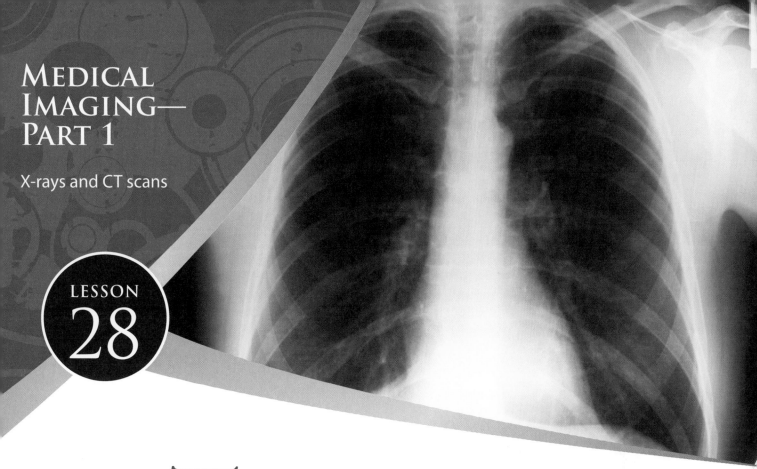

MEDICAL IMAGING— PART 1

X-rays and CT scans

What are X-rays and how do they help us?

Words to know:

medical imaging

radiography

fluoroscopy

computer axial tomography/CT scan/ CAT scan

radiology

The invention of the microscope was important to medicine because it opened a window into the world of cells and microorganisms. This technology is indispensable for many diagnostic tests. However, doctors often need to see what is going on inside the body itself. This led to the development of several technologies that together are called **medical imaging**. These technologies allow the doctor to see inside the human body without breaking the skin or causing damage to the body. There are many types of medical imaging technologies. Today, we will look at three types of imaging that all involve X-rays. In the next lesson, we will examine some methods that do not involve X-rays.

Discovery of X-rays

X-ray technology began in 1895, when a German scientist named Wilhelm Konrad von Roentgen (shown here) accidentally discovered a new type of energy. Roentgen was performing experiments with a special glass tube called a Crookes tube. He placed a glowing tube inside a black cardboard box, and then closed all the doors and the curtains on the windows to verify that no light was escaping the box. He did not see any light coming from the box; however, he did notice a glowing light across the room. A paper that had been treated with special chemicals was

Wilhelm Roentgen

glowing. The glowing stopped as soon as the tube was shut off, and began glowing again when it was turned on again. This showed that the tube was emitting some sort of invisible rays. Not knowing what the rays were, Roentgen named them X-rays, and that is what they have been called ever since.

Roentgen continued experimenting with these unseen rays and did many tests involving photographic plates. He discovered that these rays were able to pass through certain materials and unable to pass through other materials. Eventually, Wilhelm had his wife Anna place her hand over a photographic plate across from a Crookes tube and made the first X-ray of a human hand. Pictured here is a copy of that first X-ray. You can see that X-rays do not pass through bones or through metal such as the ring that was on Anna's hand. Some people failed to see the significance of Roentgen's discovery; however, many scientists quickly saw the importance and began using this new technology to view bones and other parts of the human body. Wilhelm Roentgen received the first Nobel Prize for Physics in 1901 for his discovery of the X-ray.

Use of X-rays

Today, X-ray technology is quite commonplace in medical offices around the world. What we commonly think of as having an X-ray taken is what is more properly referred to as **radiography**. A radiograph, or X-ray, is an image made by passing X-rays through a part of the body and recording the amount of energy that emerges. Dense body parts such as bones and teeth absorb nearly all of the X-ray energy that hits them. Softer, less dense materials allow most or nearly all of the X-ray to pass through. This allows an image to be made of the dense parts inside the body. Radiography is especially useful for seeing broken bones and for finding foreign particles inside the body. Dentists also use this technology to identify cavities or other problems with teeth.

Fluoroscopy

Another important imaging technology involving X-rays is called **fluoroscopy**. Fluoroscopy is used to make images of internal organs in motion. A screen that detects X-rays is placed behind the patient and X-rays are sent through the patient. In order to view the desired organ, the patient is given a barium solution, either injected into the bloodstream or swallowed into the digestive system. Barium absorbs X-rays, allowing the doctor to view the barium as it passes through the patient's body. This allows the doctor to see inside a heart or in the digestive system to find obstructions or other problems.

One of the most important uses of fluoroscopy is in treating blocked arteries in the heart. It is vital for blood to flow through the heart, but sometimes the arteries supplying blood to the heart muscle become clogged with cholesterol or other substances. This can lead to a heart attack. In the past, the only way to deal with clogged arteries was to do open heart surgery where the clogged arteries were removed and replaced with open arteries from another part of the body. While this kind of surgery is still necessary in some cases, the use of fluoroscopy has made other, less invasive treatments possible. Often the patient is injected with a barium solution and the fluoroscope is used to locate the blockage. Then a small instrument is fed into the artery through a tiny incision and removes or breaks up the clog, eliminating the need for major surgery.

CAT scans

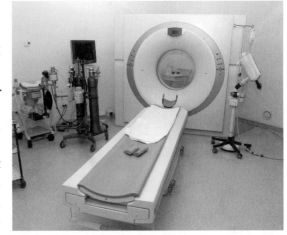

Although radiography is very useful for viewing dense or hard objects in the body, a different method was needed to view soft tissues, especially the brain. Two scientists working independently both came up with a similar idea. Sir Godfrey Hainsfield and Allan Cormack both realized that if multiple X-ray images could be made of an organ taken in just slightly different locations, that those images could be put together with the aid of a computer to show what the organ looked like. Although these men developed these ideas in the

Medical Inventions

MAKING A PICTURE FROM SLICES

Making a three dimensional image from multiple two dimensional pictures is the idea behind CT scans.

Purpose: To get a better idea of how a CT scan works

Materials: orange, knife

Procedure:

1. Slice an orange into several thin slices. Try to make at least 6 or 7 slices.

2. Place the slices flat on the table in a row, in the order that you cut them from the orange.

3. Carefully observe each slice. Each slice is similar yet different and each slice gives you a glimpse inside the orange.

4. Now carefully stack the slices on top of each other.

Conclusion: You have now formed a three dimensional orange from two dimensional slices. This is how a CT scan forms an image of the brain or other organ. However, a CT scan makes hundreds or even thousands of slices of the object so the computer can produce views of nearly any part of the organ from any side or direction.

late 1960s, computer technology did not catch up with their vision until the mid 1970s. This technology is called computer tomography, or **computer axial tomography**, and is shortened to **CAT** or **CT scanning**.

When a patient receives a CT scan, he/she lies on a flat surface while a donut-shaped X-ray tube scans the part of the body to be tested (see right). The X-ray tube takes hundreds of X-rays as it moves over the patient. The computer then compiles all of these images into a complete image of the organ being tested. This process produces amazing 3-D images of soft tissue as well as bones, allowing doctors to diagnose many problems without having to perform dangerous and painful surgery. For their invention of the CT technology, Hainsfield and Cormack shared the 1979 Nobel Prize for medicine.

Radiography, fluoroscopy, and tomography are combined into one area of medicine called **radiology**. There are many uses for radiology and all have greatly improved the lives and health of millions of people. ■

WHAT DID WE LEARN?

- How does an X-ray work?
- What are some common uses of a radiograph X-ray?
- What is fluoroscopy used for?
- What is a CT scan used for?

TAKING IT FURTHER

- How can you make a 3-dimensional image from 2-dimensional pictures?
- Which type of X-ray technology is best for viewing solid objects?
- How can X-ray technology be useful in a war hospital?
- How might X-ray technology be useful to archeologists?

X-RAYS IN INDUSTRY

Although X-ray technology has a myriad of uses in the medical field, X-rays are also used in many industrial applications as well. X-rays are used to make images of many metal parts including bridge supports, airplane engines, and other metal pieces. X-rays can reveal micro-cracks that could weaken the object. Thus, the use of X-rays helps to ensure that these items are safe. X-rays are also used for safety at airports where luggage is scanned for weapons that could be used to harm passengers. Explain how X-rays can be used to find weapons.

X-ray technology is also used for quality control in many applications. For example, X-rays can be used to determine the exact thickness of steel plates. X-rays are also used to determine if each can of soda pop is full enough. Explain how you think an X-ray can be used to test the fullness of a soda can.

X-rays can be used to identify substances in an unknown sample or to ensure that a sample contains the correct amount of each substance because each different material gives off a slightly different X-ray signature. Thus, X-rays are used for many different kinds of quality control. You can be thankful that God created X-rays and that He has allowed man to discover so many uses for them.

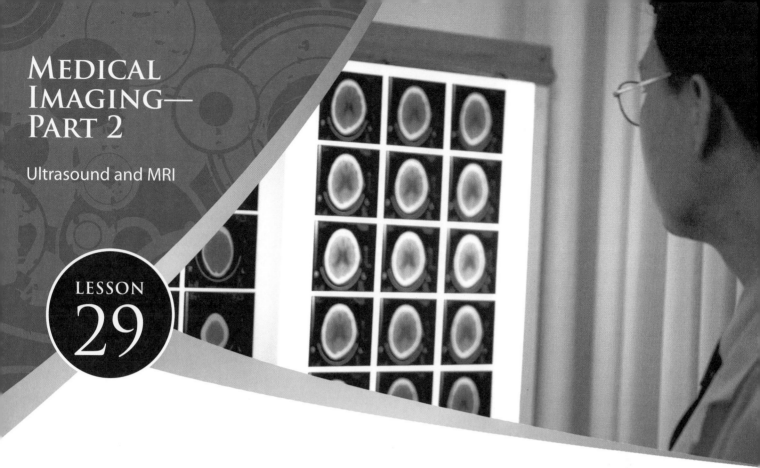

MEDICAL IMAGING— PART 2

Ultrasound and MRI

How can we see inside the body?

Words to know:

ultrasound

transducer

piezoelectric

magnetic resonance imaging/MRI

Challenge words:

Doppler ultrasound

X-ray technology is very useful for helping doctors see inside a patient without performing invasive surgery. However, X-rays can be harmful to patients as well. The radiation can damage cells. So, often other forms of medical imaging are preferable to X-rays. Ultrasound and magnetic resonance imaging (MRI) are two such technologies that help doctors see what is going on inside a patient without using potentially harmful X-rays.

Development of ultrasound

Ultrasound technology grew out of the Department of Defense's development of sonar. Just as sonar uses sound waves to detect things underwater, ultrasound uses sound waves to detect objects inside the human body. In fact, another name for an ultrasound image is a sonogram, because it uses the same technology as sonar.

An ultrasound image begins with the transducer. The transducer is an instrument that is placed on the body. It generates short pulses of sound at high frequency and then detects the echo of that signal. The transducer contains many small thin wafers that are made from a piezoelectric material. A piezoelectric material is one whose shape deforms when an electric current passes through it and also generates a current when it is deformed. Thus, when the sound wave bounces back it deforms the material and generates an electrical signal.

This electrical signal is then sent to a computer that translates that signal into a visual image. There are several factors that help determine what that image will look like. First, the time it takes for the signal to reflect back to the transducer indicates how deeply into the body the signal has traveled. Also, the strength or intensity of the signal indicates the type of body material that it reflected off of. The density of the tissue and the elasticity of the tissue both affect the amount of the signal that gets reflected. Also, the amount of signal that is reflected is affected by the shape of the surface. A flat smooth surface will reflect nearly all of the sound, while an uneven surface will scatter some of the sound. The computer takes all of this into account and generates a very useful image of the inside of the body.

The idea behind a CT scan has been employed in new ultrasound technology. Some ultrasound equipment can scan an image and generate hundreds of slices just like the CT scan does. The computer can then generate a three dimensional image from these slices.

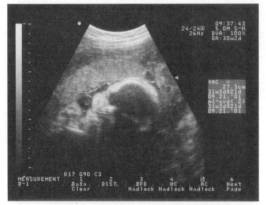

Ultrasound image of a baby

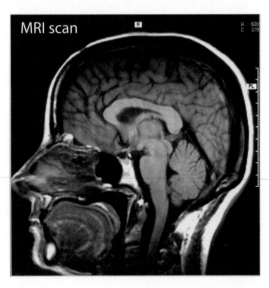

Use of ultrasound

Ultrasound is used extensively in three areas of medicine. Cardiologists often use it to study the heart and blood flow, internists use it to view the organs in the abdomen, and obstetricians use it to view babies as they are developing in the womb. Ultrasound has been used to diagnose many diseases and is safer and less costly than many other forms of diagnosis, but the application that most people are familiar with is the viewing of a baby like the one shown here. Nearly one half of all pregnant women have an ultrasound before their baby is born. An ultrasound can help a doctor determine many things about a developing baby including its approximate age (and therefore approximate due date), its gender, and any possible developmental problems. Many babies' lives have been saved because of ultrasound technology. Some problems that can be detected by ultrasound can now be corrected by microsurgery inside the womb, and other conditions can be dealt with at birth if detected ahead of time.

MRI

Another important form of medical imaging is magnetic resonance imaging, better known as MRI. MRI produces a visual image of soft tissue and internal organs by using a magnetic field. A giant magnet produces a magnetic field around the patient's body. The protons

Medical Inventions

UNDERSTANDING MAGNETIC FIELDS

Purpose: To visualize how an MRI detects changes in the nuclei of atoms

Materials: two magnets, compass, watch

Procedure:

1. Place a magnet next to a compass and watch what happens to the needle. Even though a compass needle naturally points to the earth's magnetic north, if a magnet is placed near the compass it will generate a stronger field and cause the needle to orient toward it. This is what is happening to the nuclei of the atoms in a patient's body when he is placed in the MRI's magnetic field.

2. Now place a second magnet near the compass and move it around. Watch as the needle wobbles trying to line up with the new magnetic field.

3. Remove the second magnet and see how long it takes for the needle to line back up with the first magnet. This is equivalent to the radio waves that are passed through the patient's body that cause the atoms to flip back and forth. If you had several compasses they would realign themselves in different lengths of time and the time required for all of them or a certain percentage of them to realign would vary with the number of compasses you had. This would correspond to the various times it takes for the atomic nuclei to line up in different types of tissues.

4. Now remove the first magnet. The compass needle naturally aligns itself with the earth's magnetic field. This is what happens to the patient's body when he completes the MRI process. His body returns to its natural orientation and no damage is done to the tissues that were scanned.

5. If your compass no longer points to north when the magnets are removed, you can repair it by placing the south end of a magnet on the compass and slowly drawing it up to the N on the compass several times. This should realign the compass.

in the nucleus of an atom are spinning and are electrically charged, so they act as tiny magnets. When a person is placed in the MRI's magnetic field, the protons in their body line up with the magnetic field.

A radio signal is then injected into the part of the body to be studied. This radio signal is absorbed by the atoms and causes the protons to spin differently, producing a signal that is read by the MRI machine.

Just like with the CT scan, an MRI makes hundreds or even thousands of pictures as it scans the patient. The computer then uses this information to generate an image that helps doctors diagnose a patient's problem. MRI can be performed from front to back or side to side and the computer can generate cross sections of the organ in any direction. MRI is a rather expensive procedure so it is not always the first choice, but it can sometimes

MRI scanner

Medical Inventions

diagnose a problem that cannot be detected by other methods.

Medical imaging, whether X-ray, CT scanning, ultrasound, or MRI, are all very important inventions for helping doctors make accurate diagnoses and treatments without opening up a patient to look inside. The marvelous imagination and ingenuity of the engineers and scientists who have developed these technologies demonstrates how they used the creativity given to them by God to do a great deal of good. ∎

WHAT DID WE LEARN?

- What are two forms of medical imaging that do not use X-rays?

- How does an ultrasound machine generate images?

- How does an MRI generate an image?

- Why are ultrasound and MRI preferable to X-rays in some instances?

TAKING IT FURTHER

- Why must a person undergoing an MRI remove all metal from her body?

- The newest ultrasound is sometimes referred to as 4-D ultrasound. Why do you think it is called this?

DOPPLER ULTRASOUND

Review lesson 21 on radar and sonar, and especially review the information on the Doppler effect. Using what you have learned about these technologies, explain how you think **Doppler ultrasound** could be used to view the flow of blood through the human body.

Medical Inventions

MICROSURGERY

Keeping it small

What is microsurgery?

Words to know:

microsurgery

endoscope

The goal of a doctor is to first do no harm to the patient, and then to try to help the patient as much as possible. Anytime a doctor makes an incision in a patient, he is harming the patient. Sometimes it is necessary to perform surgery to help the patient get well, but doctors are continually looking for ways to treat patients without harming them. In particular, they look for ways to treat people without cutting their bodies open. Medical imaging has provided many ways to help doctors accomplish this goal. Another advancement in medicine that makes surgery easier on patients is microsurgery.

Microsurgery can refer to any surgery that is performed with small incisions to prevent trauma to the patient. It is easier for a patient to recover from a small incision than from a large incision and there is less chance for infection as well. One way that microsurgery is performed is by allowing the doctor to view the area of the body he is working on through a microscope. This allows the doctor to see tiny parts of the body such as small blood vessels and helps him/her to make small incisions or small stitches that would be difficult to make without the aid of a microscope. In order to perform this kind of surgery, specially designed tools are needed for very precise cutting and suturing. This type of microsurgery is important for reattaching severed body parts and restoring the blood flow to them.

Another device that has been instrumental in promoting microsurgery is the endoscope. An endoscope is a very tiny camera on the end of a tube that can be inserted inside the patient. The camera sends back pictures of the inside of the body, allowing the doctor to see exactly what is going on. The endoscope is useful for diagnosis by allowing the doctor to see inside the body. An

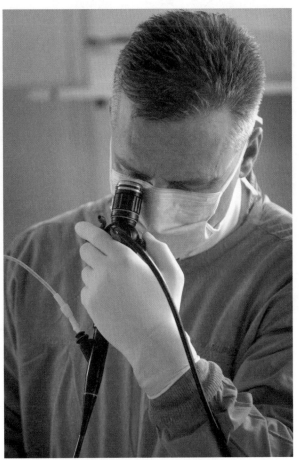

A doctor checking a patient's lungs with an endoscope.

endoscope can be inserted into a patient's throat or stomach. It can also be inserted nearly anywhere in the body through a very small incision. Thus, it is a very important tool for microsurgery.

In 1994 a special robotic arm was introduced that helped make microsurgery even more convenient. The robot, called AESOP (Automated Endoscopic System for Optimal Positioning), can hold the endoscope in place so the surgeon's hands are free to perform the surgery. AESOP can be repositioned by a foot pedal or by voice commands. Since the invention of AESOP, surgical robots have become an indispensable part of microsurgery.

All surgical robotic systems have similar components. First, they have a computer workstation that controls the robot through voice commands or remote control from the doctor; second, they contain a video display that shows the output from the camera in the endoscope; and third, they have hand controls the doctor can use to manipulate the robotic arms.

In 2000 the FDA approved a robotic surgical system called da Vinci. This system has been used for many microsurgical procedures. For example, a gallbladder operation used to require a large incision and weeks of recovery for the patient. Now, with the use of robots, a doctor makes three small incisions, smaller than the diameter of a pencil. Through one incision, a robotic arm holds the endoscope to show the surgeon the inside of the patient. Two other robotic arms hold the instruments needed for cutting, clamping, and stitching inside the patient. The doctor uses joysticks to manipulate the two arms that are holding the instruments. The doctor never actually touches the instruments, and he is seated at a console across the room where he watches the video monitor and manipulates the robotic arms.

In Germany, robotic surgery has been used to perform cardiac bypass surgery.

FUN FACT

Professor Earl Owen graduated as a surgeon from Sydney University in Australia and moved to London with a burning desire to help babies born with deformities. While trying to operate on a tiny newborn, he realized that the surgery could be so much more precise if he could use a microscope while working. He took his ideas and designs to the microscope makers Zeiss, and together they developed a range of equipment that made surgery possible on a tiny scale. In 1970, Owen performed the first microsurgery operation when he rejoined an amputated index finger.

DOING YOUR OWN MICROSURGERY

Pretend that you are a surgeon. You have two patients that are both oranges. Your oranges each need to have one of their seeds removed.

Purpose: To compare traditional surgery with microsurgery

Materials: two oranges, knife, cutting board, tweezers

Procedure:

1. On the first orange you will perform a traditional surgery. Using a knife and cutting board, cut one orange in half and remove a seed. If your orange does not have seeds, remove a portion of the stem in the middle instead.

2. Observe how much of the orange has been affected by the cut you made.

3. Next, put the two halves together and tape them so that they stay together.

4. You will perform microsurgery on the second orange. Start by cutting a small hole, about the size of a dime, through just the peel on the side of the orange.

5. Next, cut a small incision into one orange wedge and, using tweezers, remove a seed.

6. Replace any fruit that you removed. Replace the peel that you removed and tape it into place.

Questions:

• Which orange is closest to its original condition after you removed the seed?

• Which patient would theoretically have the easiest time recovering from the operation?

Conclusion: As you can see, microsurgery is generally less invasive and easier on the patient.

Traditionally, this kind of surgery is called open heart surgery and requires the chest to be opened with a very long incision down the center of the chest, revealing the heart and arteries involved in the procedure. However, with robotic surgery, only small incisions are made and the patient's recovery time is much less.

Robotic surgery has many advantages. First, the incisions are much smaller making recovery much easier. Second, robotic arms give the surgeon more control. The computer can translate a relatively large movement from the surgeon into a small movement of the robot allowing the surgeon to make very precise movements. The computer is also programmed to ignore hand tremors, so even if the surgeon

WHAT DID WE LEARN?

• What is microsurgery?

• List at least three inventions that have made microsurgery possible.

• Why is microsurgery often better than traditional surgery?

• Name three advantages to using robotic arms for microsurgery.

• What are three parts of a robotic surgical system?

TAKING IT FURTHER

• What is one disadvantage to robotic surgery?

• What might be some advantages to tele-surgery?

becomes tired, the robot remains steady. In the future, the cost of robotic surgery will likely be less than the cost of traditional surgery because fewer people are needed in the operating room during robotic or microsurgery.

With the doctor performing the surgery in a different part of the room from the patient, the question arises, "Can surgery be performed remotely?" Could the doctor be in one city and the patient in another city? The answer is, "Yes." On September 7, 2001, a doctor in New York removed the gallbladder of a patient in France. This is not a common occurrence, mostly because the time delay between computers on different sides of the world is too great for the robots to respond quickly to the doctor's commands. However, as communications and computers improve, tele-surgery is not unthinkable.

Future advances in microsurgery are sure to make surgery much safer and easier on the patient, and in the long run, it will be less costly as well. ■

DESIGN A ROBOTIC SURGERY SYSTEM

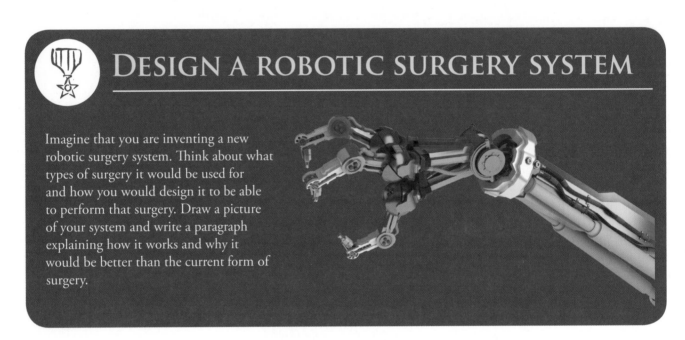

Imagine that you are inventing a new robotic surgery system. Think about what types of surgery it would be used for and how you would design it to be able to perform that surgery. Draw a picture of your system and write a paragraph explaining how it works and why it would be better than the current form of surgery.

UNIT 6

ENTERTAINMENT

◊ **Describe** how technology is used in entertainment.

◊ **Explain** how entertainment technology has developed over time.

KEY CONCEPTS | UNIT LESSONS

INVENTIONS & TECHNOLOGY 133

ROLLER COASTERS

Ahhhh!

LESSON
31

How were roller coasters invented?

Words to know:

road wheel

upstop wheel

guide wheel

Y ou listen to the clack . . . clack . . . clack as your car slowly goes up the hill. Then, just as you think you can't stand the suspense any longer, you plunge down the other side, screaming all the way! If you have ever been on a roller coaster, you know the thrill of speeding up and down hills and around curves at breathtaking speeds. The invention of the roller coaster is one of the most interesting uses of the forces of physics that man has devised.

It is believed that the roller coaster can trace its roots back to the ice hills in Russia in the 16th and 17th centuries. The Russians built wooden ramps on hills and poured water on them in the winter and then used sleds to go down the hills. People from France wanted to experience this same thrill at home, but because France does not get as cold as Russia in the winter, a different method was devised.

In 1804 the French built a ramp with tracks on it and a sled with wheels that followed the tracks. They called this hill the Russian Mountains and this is believed to be the world's first roller coaster. In 1817 a more elaborate series of tracks was built at Beaujon Gardens, and the entertainment industry of roller coasters was born.

The first known roller coaster in the United States was in a mining town in Pennsylvania, called Mauch Chunk. Originally, this was a mining railway that was used to haul coal up the mountain. The cars were pulled up the mountain by mules, and after the cars were unloaded, the mules were put into the cars and sent back down the track. When the mine was closed, someone decided that people might pay for a ride down the mountain, so in 1873 a steam engine was added to replace the mules, and America's first roller coaster was in business. The owners charged people five cents for a ride and nearly 35,000 people rode

Entertainment

the Mauch Chunk Switchback Railway the first year. This roller coaster operated until 1938.

FUN FACT

Approximately 300 million people ride roller coasters each year.

The first roller coaster built in America that was designed specifically as a ride, was built in 1884 at Coney Island, New York. Its top speed was 6 mph (2.7 m/s), but it was a hit. Roller coasters began popping up all over the country. By 1920 there were approximately 2,000 roller coasters in the United States. But with the onset of the Great Depression, people did not have money to spend on thrill rides, so roller coasters began to close. Their numbers gradually decreased until there were only about 200 coasters in the U.S. in 1960. In the last decade or so, roller coasters have experienced a revival and their numbers are again increasing.

Roller coasters operate on the basic principles of gravity and Newton's laws of motion. Once the roller coaster car is lifted to the highest hill on the track, gravity takes over and every movement is a result of momentum. The car's potential energy is converted into kinetic energy as gravity pulls it down the hill. Then the car's momentum carries it up the next hill and around the next curve. Engineers use computer models to test out designs over and over before the track is ever built. They must know not only how much energy will be needed for cars to move over the track, but they must also make sure that the highest hill provides enough additional energy to overcome the forces of friction and air resistance. They must make sure that the curves, loops, and corkscrews are designed in such a way that the passengers will have fun and feel a thrill, without experiencing so much force that it becomes uncomfortable. The very first looping roller coaster was built in 1888, but the force placed on the riders as they went around the loop was nearly 12 times the normal force of gravity, and most passengers refused to ride it a second time. Since then, engineers have learned to make loops that are teardrop shaped instead of perfectly round to reduce the force on the riders.

Early roller coasters were wooden structures that were sometimes unsafe. However, today's roller coasters are very safe. Most new coasters are built with a steel tube track and cars that have nylon wheels. This makes for a very safe and smooth ride. The cars are designed with a three wheel system. The top wheel, called the **road wheel**, bears the weight of the car and runs along the track. The bottom wheel, the

FUN FACT

At the time of publication, the world's tallest and fastest roller coaster was Kingda Ka, located at Six Flags Great Adventure in New Jersey. This mammoth coaster launches the 18-passenger train from 0 to 128 mph (57 m/s) in just under 4 seconds. The coaster train then climbs up a 456-foot (139 m) tall steel tower. Immediately it starts a terrifying vertical free fall down 418 feet (127 m), followed by a 270-degree spiral twist.

Entertainment

DESIGN YOUR OWN ROLLER COASTER

Purpose: To design and build your own model roller coaster

Materials: flexible clear tubing, small marble or BB

Procedure:

1. Using flexible clear tubing, build a track with hills, loops, and curves.

2. Place a small marble or BB in the top of the tube and see if it makes it to the end. Keep in mind that the only energy the marble has is the potential energy it has from being higher at the beginning than at the end.

3. If your marble does not make it to the end of your ride, redesign it and lower some of the hills so that the momentum will carry the marble further. Have fun and be creative.

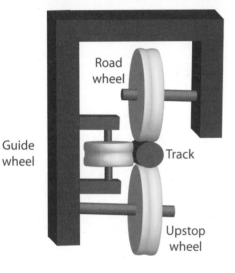

Road wheel

Guide wheel

Track

Upstop wheel

upstop wheel, keeps the car from leaving the track vertically. Finally, a sideways wheel, called the guide wheel, keeps the car from sliding sideways. This system virtually guarantees that the car will not leave the track.

Other safety features include restraints such as seat belts, lap bars, and shoulder bars, which are all designed to hold the passenger in the car. Sensors along the track continually monitor the progress of the ride and computers control the cars so that there is very little chance of a problem. The tracks contain brakes periodically that are computer controlled, so if a car needs to be stopped, it can be stopped nearly anywhere along the track. Also, roller coasters are tested extensively before they are ever opened to the public. Sand bags get to be the first passengers. If all goes well, then employees of the park are usually the next passengers. Finally, a new ride is open to the public. So, if roller coasters are your thing, you can be assured that the ride has been designed with safety and comfort in mind. ■

WHAT DID WE LEARN?

- What are the physical laws governing the operation of a roller coaster?

- What are the names of the three wheels on roller coaster cars and the purpose of each?

- What are some safety features that are built into roller coasters?

- Explain why a roller coaster car does not stop at the bottom of the first hill.

TAKING IT FURTHER

- What would happen if the first hill was not the highest hill on the track?

- Why doesn't the car have enough energy to make it to the top of a higher hill, or even one the same height, as the first one?

- What are the sources of friction in a roller coaster?

Entertainment

THE THRILL OF THE RIDE

The differing speeds and sudden turns of a roller coaster are what give you the thrill of the ride. During a ride your body can experience between three and six times the normal force of gravity at one point, and just a few seconds later, your body can experience as little as 0.2 times the force of gravity. These sudden changes in force affect your body in several different ways.

First, the forces squeeze your stomach. This is one reason some people say that rides make them feel sick. Second, the forces affect the joints of your body. Your muscles and joints contain receptors that help tell your brain where your body parts are. But if you are suddenly jerked from one position to another, your brain can get confused. But the most noticeable effect on your body is experienced by your inner ear.

Your inner ear has three semicircular canals that are filled with fluid. One canal senses forward and backward movements, one senses side to side movements, and the third senses up and down movements. Your brain senses changes in this fluid to help keep your body balanced. When you ride a roller coaster, the fluid inside your ear is sloshing all around and your brain has trouble keeping track of which way is up. This causes many people to feel dizzy and disoriented. This can add to the thrill of the ride; however, some people dislike this feeling and don't like to ride roller coasters or other rides.

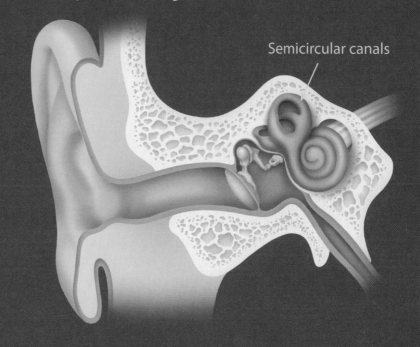

Semicircular canals

Purpose: To appreciate how your brain and your inner ear work together

Materials: None

Procedure:

1. Close your eyes and stand on one foot. You will notice your body trying to compensate to keep you balanced. Even though you can't see when you are no longer standing straight, your brain can sense the movement of your body by the change in the levels of fluid in your inner ear.

2. Now, with your eyes closed, spin around in a circle for a few seconds. Keep your eyes closed when you stop. How do you feel? Do you feel dizzy?

Conclusion: You feel dizzy because the fluid in your ear is still spinning when you suddenly stop. Your brain thinks your body is still moving even though it isn't. This causes you to feel dizzy until the liquid in your ear stops and your brain catches up with where your body really is. This is similar to what is happening to you when you are on a roller coast ride—only the changes are more sudden.

PHONOGRAPH

Listen to that sound

What is a phonograph and how does it work?

Words to know:

phonograph

When you consider inventions that have been developed for entertainment, you have to consider those developed specifically to bring us sound recordings. The sound recording business is one of the largest entertainment industries in the world. And all of this was due to the man most famous for the invention of the electric light bulb—Thomas Edison.

You may not associate CDs and MP3 players with the electric light or the telephone, but that is where it all began. We discussed earlier how Alexander Graham Bell invented the telephone. But of course, the development of the telephone did not stop there. Thomas Edison looked at Bell's design and decided to improve it. Edison was hard of hearing and wanted a telephone in which the voices could be easily heard. Bell's original design did not amplify the voice and it was often difficult to hear the speaker, so Edison went to work on this problem and designed a better speaker for the phone, which greatly improved the sound quality of the receiver. While working on this device, Edison thought of the idea of recording the sound of a human voice in some way and then playing it back at a later time. He called this device a phonograph.

In 1877 Edison drew up the plans for a phonograph and gave them to John Kruesi, the manager of his machine lab. Kruesi worked on the parts for four days and presented Edison with the model he had asked for. This design included a hand-cranked cylinder covered with foil, a mouth piece, a metal disk called a diaphragm, and a needle. As one spoke into the mouthpiece, the diaphragm would vibrate, causing the needle to move. The person speaking would crank the handle, thus turning the cylinder. The needle movements would be recorded in the foil on the cylinder. The cylinder could then be rewound and the needle connected to a speaker. The needle would follow the grooves made in the cylinder and change them back into sound.

Edison called several of his coworkers into his office and demonstrated the phonograph as he spoke into the mouthpiece of his new invention. He recorded the nursery rhyme "Mary Had a Little Lamb," and his coworkers were astounded to hear the device work the first time it was tested. Edison immediately recognized the advantages of this device for dictation and even made a miniature version to place inside a talking doll.

Edison then turned his attention to working on the electric light bulb. While he was doing this, Charles Bell, a cousin of Alexander Graham Bell, improved the phonograph by replacing the foil cylinders with wax cylinders. Edison later improved on Bell's design. Although Edison invented the phonograph with dictation in mind, people quickly began demanding entertainment recordings. Edison was never a man to turn away from what the public demanded, so he started producing cylinders with recordings of popular music and the recording industry was born.

Since Edison's time, recording devices have changed drastically. In 1884 Emile Berliner introduced the gramophone, which used flat zinc disks instead of wax cylinders. Eventually, recordings were made on vinyl records. In 1948 Columbia Records produced the first long-play vinyl record, similar to the one shown here, which could hold several songs on each side. Vinyl records were the most popular way to listen to music for many decades.

In 1934 magnetic tapes were first used for radio broadcasts. By the 1960s magnetic tapes became very popular for recording and playing back music and other sound recordings offered to the general public. Magnetic tapes use a very different technology from phonographs. In a tape recorder, the sound is converted into current that passes through an electromagnet. This creates a small magnetic field. This magnetic field is stored in the magnetic material on a tape. When the tape is passed through the electromagnetic field of a tape player, the magnetic field on the tape causes current to flow through the player. This current is translated into sound waves and is heard through the speaker. Tape players are more portable than vinyl records so they quickly replaced record players in many applications.

Then, in 1983 a new type of disk was developed by the Sony and Philips companies. The compact disk, or CD, was invented. CDs use digital technology, and thus have improved sound quality. The exact sound wave is stored on vinyl records and magnetic tapes. This is called an analog recording. However, CDs do not store an exact version of the sound wave. Instead, the sound wave is converted into a binary code of 1s and 0s. This is called a digital recording. Digital recordings can produce a better sound than analog recordings because they do not pick up distortion or interference, and they do not degrade over time.

MAKING A CD MODEL

Recall that a CD player works by shining a laser on a series of pits burned into the surface of the CD. The pits do not reflect the light, whereas the flat areas do reflect the light.

Purpose: To see how a CD player works

Materials: aluminum foil, scissors, cardboard, flashlight or laser pen

Procedure:

1. In a line, cut a series of rectangles that are approximately one inch high and varying lengths into a piece of aluminum foil. They can be as short as ½ inch or as long as two inches. Make some holes closer together than others.

2. Place the foil over a piece of cardboard. This is your CD model.

3. Take your model and a flashlight or laser pen into a dark room.

4. Place the CD model on a flat surface where you can stand with your eyes looking straight down on the foil.

5. Slowly scan the flashlight beam across the code.

Conclusion: Notice how the beam is brightly reflected by the foil but is dimly reflected by the cardboard. This is how a CD reader determines the digital code for the recording. On an actual CD, the holes are obviously much smaller and the laser beam is much narrower than your flashlight beam, but the process is basically the same.

A compact disk is a small disk covered with a reflective material. A laser is used to burn pits into the surface of the disk along a very narrow track that starts in the center of the disk and spirals outward. The pits that are burned into the disk represent the 0s, and areas that are left flat, or are not burned, represent 1s. A CD is then placed into a player that shines a laser light onto the CD. A detector senses reflected light from the disk. Where the surface is flat, representing a 1, the light reflects back. Where there is a pit, representing a 0, the light is scattered, so the sensor can detect the pattern of 1s and 0s that has been recorded. The player then translates this pattern into sound and sends it through the speaker. This same technology has been used not only for sound recordings, but also for data storage on computers and digital video disks (DVDs) for movies.

With the constant demand for music in our society, the recording industry will continue to find ways to provide recordings in more convenient forms. ∎

WHAT DID WE LEARN?

- What is a phonograph?
- Who invented the first phonograph?
- Which devices were later developed from the idea of the phonograph?
- What recording technology uses electromagnets?

TAKING IT FURTHER

- What are some advantages of CDs over vinyl records?
- List at least three devices that use the idea of changing sound into a different form, then changing it back again.
- Other than entertainment, what are some uses for recording and playing back sound?

Entertainment

MP3 PLAYERS

Computers have played a big part in changing the recording industry. Not only do computers make it easier to make quality recordings for CDs, but computers make it possible to take the digital signal from a CD and convert it into a compressed format for an MP3 player. The MP3 format compresses the data so that it takes up less space. For example, a four minute song in regular CD format takes up about 40 megabytes of memory, but in MP3 format the same song takes up only 4 megabytes of memory. Thus, you can store approximately 10 times as many songs in the same amount of memory if you store them in MP3 format.

In order to listen to your MP3 player, you first load a CD into the CD drive of your computer. You select the songs you want to listen to and a computer program takes the digital signal off of the CD and converts it into MP3 format. The converted files are stored on your computer's hard drive. Then you can load the files from your hard drive into the memory of your MP3 player. Depending on how much memory your MP3 player has, you may be able to store hundreds, or even thousands, of songs.

MP3 players can record music from sources other than CDs. You can download music directly from the Internet to your MP3 player. Also, some players can record from the radio and from a microphone. Many newer MP3 players have a video screen, so you can watch movies and music videos as well as listen to music. So an MP3 player is very versatile in addition to being very small and convenient.

Based on what you have learned about communication devices and

recording devices, draw a diagram showing what parts you think need to be inside an MP3 player and explain what each part does.

MOVING PICTURES

You ought to be in pictures!

How are movies made?

Words to know:

persistence of vision

perceived motion

kinetograph/
kinetoscope

Challenge words:

computer animation

claymation

One of the most popular forms of entertainment today is going to see a movie. The motion picture business is a multi-billion dollar industry. But the first moving pictures were invented only a little more than 100 years ago, and the motion picture industry was started by none other than Thomas Edison. I hope you are starting to see by now that Edison was involved in much more than just light bulbs.

To really understand the making of movies, you must first realize that a moving picture is not truly a moving image. What we call a movie is really a series of still images that are just slightly different from each other. These images flash in front of your eyes quickly enough that your brain blends the images together in a smooth transition.

In 1824 an English doctor named P. M. Roget proposed the idea that a person's brain continues to see an image for a short period of time after the image is gone. This idea is called persistence of vision. Your brain retains an image for about 1/30th of a second, depending on how bright the image is. Within ten years of proposing this idea, many people began working on moving pictures. Today, there is some controversy over the role that persistence of vision plays in perceived motion. Some people believe that observed motion in movies is purely a psychological response, an illusion, rather than a physical phenomenon between the eyes and the brain. Regardless of why people perceive these images as moving, we know that if the images are flashed fast enough, people do perceive moving pictures.

Inventors around the world worked on various methods for making motion pictures. In 1889 Thomas Edison said that he wanted to create a device that did for the eye what the phonograph did for the ear. Edison called his camera a **kinetograph** because it recorded movements. His projector was called a **kinetoscope**. The first projected movie display was conducted by Edison in 1891. Only one person at a time could view the movie through his special projector. Later, Edison developed a system that projected an image that could be seen by multiple viewers at one time.

About the same time that Edison was working on movies in America, two brothers in France, Auguste and Louise Lumière, were working on a camera and projector system which they called a *cinematographe*. This system recorded images on celluloid and played them back. The Lumières showed the first public movie to multiple viewers in 1895. Several other inventors were working on similar inventions throughout Europe and America at this time.

In 1893 Thomas Edison built the first motion picture studio. It was a small building which his associates dubbed the "Black Maria" (ma-RYE-ah) because it was dark and cramped like a police paddy wagon that was nicknamed a black maria. The roof of the building opened up to let in sunlight, and the entire building was built on a circular track so it could be rotated with the sun to keep the light the same throughout the whole filming process. Most of the early movies that Edison made were only 20 to 30 seconds long. These movies

Edison's "Black Maria"

showed many different activities including acrobats, boxers, and ballet dancers. One of his most famous early movies showed a man sneezing.

Edison's camera would have been no good if it weren't for the invention of clear

Entertainment

MAKING YOUR OWN "MOVIE"

Purpose: To make your own moving pictures

Materials: two or more copies of the "Movie Frames" worksheet, pen or pencil, scissors, stapler

Procedure:

1. Draw a picture in each frame of the "Movie Frames" worksheet that is very similar but slightly different from the previous picture. Each square represents a frame for your movie. Do not try to make it too complicated. For example, you could draw a hand dropping a ball and show the hand in about the same position but the ball in a slightly different position in each frame. Make at least 16 different pictures.

2. After you are done drawing the pictures, cut the squares apart and stack them in order.

3. Staple the pictures together at the top or the side and flip through the pictures. If you flip through them quickly enough, it will appear that the images are moving.

film. The film used by Edison's camera was developed by the Eastman Company in 1889. This was the first commercially available clear roll film. In 1904 the Lumières patented the first color photography process.

Early films were in black and white and had no sound. Sound was added to films by 1910, and by the 1940s many films were shot in color. For the past 100 years, continuous improvements have been made to the picture and sound quality of the motion picture. Improvements in cameras, projectors, recording systems, and sound systems have all led to the giant motion picture industry we have today. ■

WHAT DID WE LEARN?

• What is a motion picture?

• Who were some of the first people to make moving pictures?

• What is persistence of vision?

TAKING IT FURTHER

• How did the phonograph influence the development of movies?

• Why did the Black Maria have a roof that could be opened?

COMPUTER ANIMATION

Computer animation plays a huge role in many movies today. With increasing demand for special effects, computers are now used to create scenes that would be impossible to film with a camera. As computers have increased in speed and power, many movies are now being completely or mostly created inside the computer instead of in front of a camera.

Computer animation starts with a frame of the object or person. This is like a skeleton or wire model of the object. Then other parts are added such as muscles and skin, giving the object its form. Finally, details such as shading and texture are added, until the computer-generated object looks very real. There are computer programs that can move the computer-generated object in many different ways. So the computer actually generates the object, moves it, and records the images to generate the movie.

Some programs allow you to do simple animations at home. But to achieve the quality of movie animation requires very expensive computers and very expensive software programs.

A simple way to achieve animation without the use of a computer is through claymation. **Claymation** uses characters or objects that are made from clay. These objects are photographed, then they are moved slightly and photographed again. This is done over and over again. Then the pictures are put together and shown very quickly to give the illusion of movement. If the changes are small enough and there are enough pictures, it can appear to the viewer that the clay object is actually moving on its own. If you have a camera and modeling clay, try making your own claymation video.

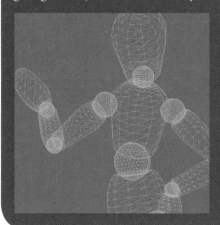
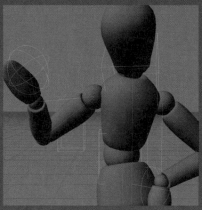

BECOMING AN INVENTOR: FINAL PROJECT

You could be the next Thomas Edison.

LESSON 34

How can I become an inventor?

People are very creative. God has given us imagination, reasoning, curiosity, and a desire to make new things. Because of this, mankind has continued to solve problems in new and inventive ways throughout history. Inventions are by no means a new thing. The ancient Egyptians invented ways to build giant pyramids, the Romans invented amazing aqueducts to carry water, and the Greeks had Greek fire, a burning liquid weapon. You can be an inventor, too.

Inventors can be men or women, girls or boys. And inventions can come about in many different ways. However, most inventions come about by following a few simple steps. First, you need to identify a problem. There is no reason to invent something that doesn't help someone in some way. Second, you need an idea for how to solve the problem. Third, you need to investigate and find out what other people have done in this area. Why reinvent the wheel (or the printing press, or the computer)?

Once you have an idea of what you want to do, you need a plan. Think about how you will solve the problem. What will your invention look like? How will it work? Next, you need to create your invention. Make a model of your invention. It doesn't have to be a beautiful finished version, but it needs to have all the working parts so you can see if it really does what you want it to do. Next, test your invention to make sure it really works. If it does, you can apply for a patent so no one else can use your idea without your permission. Finally, you need to decide what you want to do with your invention. Do you want to manufacture and sell it? Do you want to sell the idea to someone else? Do you want to improve on the invention?

Getting the idea for an invention is sometimes hard and sometimes easy, but actually making it work can often be the most difficult part. Remember how many different materials Edison and his men tried before they found the right material for the light bulb? They tried over 1,600 different materials before they got one to work. So you have to have determination to be an inventor.

If you want to be a good inventor, there are some other skills that would help you as well. Drawing well is a great advantage for an inventor. You will need to be able to draw sketches of what you want to build. Your sketches may need to be read by someone else, so they need to be clear enough for someone else to follow. Also, writing down your ideas and keeping a notebook is an important part of being a good inventor. Notebooks help you organize your thoughts and keep track of what you have tried and how well it works. If you don't write anything down, you are likely to forget what you have done and repeat the same mistakes. Also, notebooks will help those who come after you to improve on your ideas. Finally, your notebook can help you verify your work when applying for a patent.

The steps of being a good inventor are very similar to the steps of the scientific method. Briefly, the steps of the scientific method are:

1. Learn about a topic.

2. Ask a question.

3. Make a hypothesis (a good guess).

4. Design an experiment to test your hypothesis. Collect data.

5. Draw conclusions. (Does the data support your hypothesis?)

MAKING YOUR OWN INVENTION

Get a notebook and start brainstorming about possible new inventions. Look at nature. Observing how birds fly helped people understand how airplanes could fly. Look at people. What do they do? What do they struggle with? What do they spend a lot of time on? This could give you ideas for new inventions. Read the newspaper. What are people complaining about? Can you think of a way to solve the problem? Remember that you have a limited budget and that you have limited access to tools and machinery, so you might want to start with a simple invention.

If you need an idea, consider the following:

- Invent a new game

- Improve an existing invention (maybe a better mousetrap?)

- Invent a new business idea

- Invent something for the kitchen

Once you have an idea, write it down and draw several sketches of it. Explain how you expect it to work. Once you have a clear idea of how the invention will work, collect the necessary materials and build it. Try it out. If it doesn't work the way

you think it should, try to figure out why and then figure out a way to fix the problem. Be sure to record what you do and your results in your notebook.

Once you are done, show it to someone. Sharing your ideas is always fun.

Entertainment

So being an inventor is being a good scientist. The only real difference is that, as an inventor, your goal is to create something useful, but as a scientist your goal may be just to understand how something works without inventing something new. So put on your thinking caps, fire up your imaginations, and get busy inventing! ■

WHAT DID WE LEARN?

- What are the steps to inventing something?
- How is the scientific method similar to the process for inventing something?
- How are the two processes different?

TAKING IT FURTHER

- What can you do to become a better inventor?

RESEARCH PAPER

Choose an invention that was not covered in this book and do a research paper on how it works and how it was invented. Select from the suggestions below or come up with your own idea:

Cotton gin	Gas mask	Computer compiler	Zipper
Reaper	Steel	Lawn mower	Integrated circuit
Model train	Alarm clock	Safety pin	Satellite

Entertainment

CONCLUSION

God made you creative

LESSON

35

God is the great Inventor!

God is the greatest inventor of all time. Colossians 1:16 says, "For by Him [Jesus] all things were created that are in heaven and that are on earth, visible and invisible, whether thrones or dominions or principalities or powers. All things were created through Him and for Him." Look at all the things God invented. He made space, planets, stars, and moons. God designed all of the different plants and animals. God created the laws of physics. He invented chemical reactions. And God designed the human body, which may be the greatest invention of all. Read Romans 1:20. This passage tells us that God has chosen to reveal His qualities through what He has created. These qualities include His divine nature and His eternal power. We must reflect on what we see in nature and look for God's qualities. When we do, we will be in awe of God's mighty power and will worship Him.

REFLECTING ON GOD'S INVENTIONS

Divide a sheet of paper into two columns. In the first column, make a list of some of the things that God has invented. Try to be more specific than the list above. In the second column, list some of the inventions that man has come up with that mirror or use similar ideas to God's creations. Man can never invent anything more awesome than what God has created, but we can learn from what God shows us and benefit from that. ■

Entertainment

GLOSSARY

Abacus   Mechanical device using beads to perform mathematical calculations

Achromatic lens   Lens that eliminates distortion

Acoustic communication sonar   Sends and receives sound waves in code for communication

Active sonar   Generates and detects sound waves

Agitator   Device with fins for moving clothing around inside a washing machine

Airfoil   Shape whose top surface is rounded and thus longer than the bottom surface

Alternative fuel vehicle   A vehicle that does not use a petroleum product as fuel

Amplifier   Device to boost the strength of an electrical signal

Amplitude modulation/AM   Amplitude or height of the carrier signal is modified to fit the original signal

Analog   Continuous signal

Arc lighting   Light produced when electricity passes between carbon rods

Ballast   Material carried for the purpose of changing the weight of a vehicle

Ballista   Giant cross-bow

Ballistics   Study of objects moving through the air

Bernoulli's principle   As a fluid increases in velocity it decreases in pressure

Buoyancy   Force exerted by liquids and gases equal to mass of displaced fluid

Cathode Ray Tube/CRT   Phosphor coated tube that translates electrical signals into pictures

Central processing unit/CPU   Part of computer that performs most of the calculations and controls other parts of the computer

Chronometer   Clock used for navigation

Combustion   A quick burning or explosion of fuel

Compound microscope   Microscope with two lenses

Compression stroke   Second stroke that compresses the air/fuel mixture

Computer axial tomography/CAT/CT scan   Using multiple X-rays to form a 3-dimensional image of internal organs

Cryogenic fuel   Fuel that is liquid only at extremely low temperatures under great pressure

Crystal oscillator   Material that vibrates at a very precise rate when electricity flows through it

Digital   Series of pulses

Dive planes   Wing-like attachments to the sides of a submarine for stability and diving

Drag   Backward force generated by friction with air molecules

Drawbridge   Bridge that splits and can be lifted up to allow traffic to pass beneath the bridge

Duplex telegraph   Telegraph that could send two messages as once

Electron microscope   Device that uses a beam of electrons and magnetic coils to view magnified images

Elevated train   Train that travels on rails built above the ground

Endoscope   Device with a very tiny camera at the end of a flexible tube

Exhaust stroke   Fourth stroke that pushes out any unburned fuel and gases that resulted from the combustion

Eyepiece   Top lens of microscope

Facsimile/FAX   An exact copy

Fluoroscopy   Making images of internal organs by using X-rays to track the movement of an X-ray absorbing material

Frequency modulation/FM   Frequency of the carrier signal is modified to fit the original signal

Guide wheel   Sideways wheel of roller coaster—prevents cars from sliding sideways

Hard drive   Device storing information in magnetic fields or long term memory

Hardware   Parts of computer you can actually touch

Heat   Energy in the movement of molecules

Hovercraft   Air cushioned vehicle that travels over a cushion of air

Hull   Outside shell of a ship

Hypergolic fuel   Fuel composed of two chemicals that ignite when they come in contact with each other

Incandescence   Light produced when current is passed through certain materials

Inert gas   Element that does not easily react chemically with other elements

Intake stroke   First stroke of an internal combustion engine that takes in fuel mixed with air

Keystone   Stone at the top of an arch bridge

Kinetograph and kinetoscope   Devices for recording and playing back moving images; called a cinematographe by Auguste and Louise Lumière

Lift   Upward force generated by air flowing faster over the top of a wing than under it

Liquid crystal display/LCD/Plasma display   Flat panel screen with liquid or plasma that responds to electrical signals

Magnetic resonance imaging/MRI   Use of magnetic fields to generate an image inside the body

Medical imaging   Technology that give a view of the inside of the body

Microphone   Device to translate sound waves into electrical signals

Microsurgery   Surgery performed with small incisions

Microwaves   Electromagnetic waves of energy

Modulation   Message is added to a carrier signal

Morse code   Code using long and short signals to represent letters

Objective   Bottom lens of microscope

Oxidizer   Material that supplies oxygen for combustion

Passive sonar   Only detects sound waves

Perceived motion   The idea that the brain sees an image moving even though the image is actually a series of still images

Persistence of vision   The brain continues to see an image for approximately 1/30th of a second after the image is removed

Phonograph   Device for recording and playing back sound

Piezoelectric   Material whose shape deforms when current passes through it

Pitch   Movement of airplane up and down as it moves forward

Pixel/Picture element   One dot or piece of information on a CRT

Platen   Thick piece of flat wood used to press the paper against the letters

Power stroke   Third stroke that forces the piston down as the fuel explodes

Proof   Quick copy to check for mistakes

Propellant   Combination of rocket fuel and oxidizer in a rocket engine

RAM   Random access memory or short term memory

Radar   RAdio Detection And Ranging—Use of radio waves to detect objects

Radiography   Making an image by passing X-rays through the body

Radiology   Area of medicine using X-ray technology

Refrigerant   Material used for state or phase changes in refrigerators

Refrigeration   The removal of heat

Resolution   The number of pixels or pieces of information that an image is broken into

Road wheel   Top wheel of roller coaster—bears weight of the cars

Roll   Movement of airplane wings tipping side to side

Rudder   Paddle at back of ship for steering

Satellite   Anything in a regular orbit around the earth

Scanning tunneling microscope/STM   Device using electrical current to measure surface of a tiny object

Screw   Propeller for moving a submarine

Simple microscope   Microscope with only one lens

Software   Electronic information stored or passed through a computer

Sonar   SOund Navigation And Ranging—Use of sound waves to detect objects

Space probe   Scientific instruments sent to explore objects in space

Submarine   Underwater vehicle

Subway   Train that travels underground

Telegram   Message sent by telegraph

Telegraph key   Metal switch for completing an electrical circuit

Telegraph receiver   Device containing an electromagnet making an audible click when current flows through it

Thermostat   Device used to regulate temperature

Thrust   Power needed to move an aircraft forward

Transducer   Device that generates pulses of sound

Treadle   Device for moving wheels of sewing machine by foot

Truss bridge   Bridge that uses a series of triangles to spread out the force

Tuner   Device to select the desired signal

Turbine   Series of blades that turn when hot gases push against them

Ultrasound   Use of sound waves to see inside the body

Upstop wheel   Bottom wheel of roller coaster—keeps car on the track

Vectored thrust system   Engine system that can direct the gases out of the engine in any direction

Weight   Downward force generated by gravity

Yaw   An airplane turning right or left

CHALLENGE GLOSSARY

Boyle's law   When a gas is compressed its volume decreases proportionally and its temperature increases proportionally to the pressure applied

Claymation   Use of clay objects in different poses to create moving pictures

Computer animation   Use of computers to make moving pictures

Doppler effect   Frequency of light and sound waves changes as the object moves toward or away from you

Doppler radar   Radar that uses change in frequency to determine the speed and direction that an object is moving

Doppler ultrasound   Use of sound waves to detect moving objects inside the body

Fiber optics   Cable consisting of hundreds of tiny glass tubes that transmit pulses of light

First-class lever   Lever with the fulcrum between the effort and the weight

Fluorescent bulbs   Bulbs filled with a gas that becomes a plasma when current is passed through it

Font   Different styles of letters

Halogen bulbs   Incandescent bulbs filled with halogen gas

Hydrofoil   Boat with airfoil shaped wings underneath that create lift as the boat moves through the water

Light-emitting diode/LED   Bulb made of semi-conducting material

Lubricant   Material that reduces friction

Magnetic levitation/Maglev   Use of repelling magnets to move a train

Newton's third law of motion   For every action the is an equal and opposite reaction

Resonance   The natural frequency at which something vibrates

Rifled   Gun barrel with a spiraling groove

Second-class lever   Lever with the weight between the fulcrum and the effort

Shuttle   Device for carrying one thread through other treads

Smooth bore   Gun barrel that is smooth and polished inside

Submersible   Submarine designed to operate at deep level of the ocean

Third-class lever   Lever with the effort between the weight and the fulcrum

V-2 rocket   Rocket designed by Germany for use in World War II

Index